A TEACHER'S GUIDE TO SPECIAL NEEDS

A Positive Response To The 1981 Education Act

A TEACHER'S GUIDE TO SPECIAL NEEDS

A Positive Response To The 1981 Education Act

Jonathan Solity
Edward Raybould

Open University Press

Milton Keynes • Philadelphia

Open University Press
12 Cofferidge Close
Stony Stratford
Milton Keynes MK11 1BY, England
and
242 Cherry Street
Philadelphia, PA 19106, USA

First Published 1988

British Library Cataloguing in Publication Data

Solity, Jonathan
A teacher's guide to special needs :
a positive response to the 1981 Education Act.
1. England. Special education. Law :
Education Act 1981. Implementation
I. Title II. Raybould, Edward
344.204'791

ISBN 0-335-15843-9
ISBN 0-335-15842-0 Pbk

Library of Congress Cataloguing-in-Publication Data

Solity, Jonathan.
    A teacher's guide to special needs: a positive response to the
1981 Education Act/Jonathan Solity, Edward Raybould.
    p.   cm.
    Bibliography: p.
    Includes index.
    1. Special education—Great Britain. 2. Great Britain. Education
Act (1981) 3. Mainstreaming in education—Great Britain.
I. Raybould, E. C.   II. Title.
LC3986. G7S65 1988
371.9'0941—dc19   88-2865 CIP
ISBN 0-335-15843-9.   ISBN 0-335-15842-0 (pbk)

Editorial and Production Services by
Fisher Duncan Ltd, 10 Barley Mow Passage, London W4 4PH
Printed in Great Britain by Oxford University Press

CONTENTS

CHAPTER SIX ASSESSMENT-THROUGH-TEACHING

CHAPTER SEVEN THE STATUTORY ASSESSMENT PROCEDURE

PREFACE

At the time of writing this book, the 1981 Education Act had been in operation for about four years. This may seem a long time to some, though we should perhaps remind ourselves of the time scale required to observe substantial effects and changes following government legislation, particularly in the education field.

Our own appreciation is that local education authorities and schools are still in the process of assimilating the Act and its attendant circulars, and working on the best ways to implement the proposals, within their respective local contexts. We make no apologies for the timing of this book therefore, as the issues are very much 'here and now'. We are also aware that such an important piece of legislation will continue to influence special educational practice for many years to come.

Many other legislative changes are also in preparation at this time with far-reaching implications. We would earnestly hope that the best features of the 1981 Act, what we have referred to in this book, as the 'spirit' of the Act will not, as a result, be relegated to a position of lesser importance. Our children, particularly those with special needs, deserve better.

Our broad intention in writing this book is conveyed in the two parts of our title. Whilst attitudes and practice regarding children with educational difficulties have been continually developing, the appearance of the recent legislation marks a significant and explicit stage in the process. We have tried therefore to 'unpack' the essential principles and requirements of the Act and accompanying documents, and to interpret and comment upon these, in the light of current, *positive* trends in special education and educational psychology.

In serving this dual aim we have presented the legislation and procedures as accurately as possible. We have also tried to draw out, in good faith, what we regard as the 'spirit' of the legislation. Beyond this, the comments and interpretations are very much our own opinions and responsibility.

We trust that the resulting framework we have produced will go some way to enabling teachers (and other allied professionals who are interested) to re-evaluate their practice with special needs children in the light of the legislation and continue to develop positive approaches to such children in their own classrooms and local authorities.

Our underlying view is that all children are special. We believe that the Act, whilst placing the focus on a small minority of children, prompts us also to think about how we provide for the *continuum* of educational needs in our schools.

AUTHORS' NOTE

In examples which are based on real life situations, names have been
altered to protect the anonymity of those concerned. Thoughout this
book male and female titles and names, and the words 'she' and 'he' are
used interchangeably.

ACKNOWLEDGEMENTS

In preparing this book we have very much appreciated the helpful
comments and suggestions on the manuscript from the following
teachers, educational psychologists and LEA advisors: David Bethell,
Maureen Glover, Bob Hart, Cynthia Hughes, Jenny Lupton, Ann
Nelson, Chris Reeve, Mark Solity and Dave Traxson. We would also
wish to acknowledge the teachers and psychologists, too many to name,
with whom we have had the pleasure of working and from whom we
have learned so much.

The authors would like to thank Routledge and Kegan Paul for
permission to reprint Table 2.3 on page 10, from Tomlinson, S. (1982)
A Sociology of Special Education.

Special thanks are due to Pia Mack for her excellent illustrations,
Danny Phillips for his help with diagrams and to our partners Sue and
Helen for their patience during our late night labours.

Finally, our sincere thanks go to Lyn Beddowes for her admirable
decoding skills and excellent typing.

Notwithstanding the help and support we received when writing this
book, the responsibility for its content and any errors remain entirely
our own.

Chapter One

INTRODUCTION

The 1981 Education Act received Royal Assent on 30th October 1981 and came into force on 1st April 1983. It makes provision with respect to children with special educational needs and marks, through government legislation, the culmination of several years discussion and debate over the nature of special education.

The Act reflects much current thinking and conventional wisdom in the area of special education. It enshrines principles of effective practice, that if implemented, will help improve the quality of education available to meet children's special needs.

The Act is one piece of educational legislation with which every primary and secondary teacher in England, Wales and Northern Ireland may well have some involvement at some time during their teaching careers. Each year new laws are passed which influence our lives, of which we are rarely aware unless of course we have a particular interest or unfortunate experience. It would be regrettable if the 1981 Act achieved similar status.

The reaction of many when first reading the Act and its associated documents was one of cautious optimism. It appeared to embody much that is desirable in special education but as time passed and the minutiae of its contents were more fully understood, less favourable opinions were expressed. It is perhaps inevitable that the more we, as lay people, acquaint ourselves with aspects of the law, what we may initially have seen as clear-cut, unambiguous statements take on a different hue. The certainties become open to more interpretations than we had first considered. We would not need lawyers and barristers if the laws of the land were any less complex than this.

In short therefore, the Act has been viewed by some as a positive step forward and by others, less favourably. Some say it goes too far, others not far enough. In either case, what can be detected is a certain spirit underlying the Act. It incorporates a framework and makes provision, in principle at least, for a notable advancement in the practice of special education.

It is this spirit that we hope to capture in this book. Our interpretation is unashamedly positive, since no matter how sceptical we may sometimes feel, we would prefer to believe, even at the risk of being naive, that the Act came into being to help improve the quality of education for children with special needs, rather than for more Machiavellian or political motives.

Even more to the point, continuing to express dissatisfaction with the

Act and criticising its contents will not achieve the desired changes, certainly in the short term. The Act is currently in force and will influence the lives of children. Whilst the present legislation may not be to everyone's liking, the reality is that the government has dictated the broad rules of the game and firmly fixed the goal posts in position, though we might wish that they had provided some of the equipment.

On a more optimistic note is the potential scope which the Act offers for making a positive contribution to children's education. Recent trends in special education in the UK and the USA have been widely welcomed. They represent a shift in thinking which would limit the tendency to think of some pupils as 'handicapped' and others as 'normal'. Now parents, teachers, advisers and administrators are encouraged to see all children as *individuals* and to focus on their *individual* needs.

There are undeniable ambiguities in the Act and its related Circulars which may lead to scepticism and caution on the part of those responsible for implementing the principles and procedures. In later chapters, we examine what to us are some of the more obvious omissions and contradictions but set this discussion within the context of deriving positive principles for future practice.

This chapter starts by introducing some of the new language that is becoming an increasing part of everyday educational life and then identifies some of the issues that may be uppermost in the minds of many readers of this book.

THE NEW LANGUAGE

Developments in any field of activity are invariably accompanied by a special vocabulary. To listen to children's conversations highlights the impact of new technology on everyday life. They discuss the latest 'Walkman' to appear on the market, computer games and the video they are going to watch later in the day. Previous generations might have been more concerned with what was on the radio and organising trips to the cinema. Similarly, recent developments in kitchen gadgetry have brought an entirely new vocabulary to domestic life.

The Education Act has also introduced new terminology to the world of education. Terms such as 'special needs', 'advice' and 'statements', have particular importance now through their use within the legislation. A phrase such as 'children with learning difficulties' which has been used frequently in the past to describe a wide range of pupils, has now acquired a more specific meaning in its use within the Act. The same is also true of the terms 'special need' and 'special educational provision'.

What perhaps needs to be remembered now is that much of the language of special education has both a legal status as well as a meaning acquired through everyday use. However, what can be confusing is establishing the way in which these terms are being employed. Their meaning, together with that of other phrases, will be explained when discussion concentrates on the details of the Act and its accompanying documentation.

WHAT DO TEACHERS ASK ABOUT THE ACT?

The 1981 Education Act has already come to the attention of many teachers in mainstream education, particularly those working within the primary sector. It has been the subject of many LEA and HMI in-service courses and generated an increasing number of articles and books.

Despite this, however, teachers with whom we have had contact have frequently raised similar questions when discussion has focused on the Act. Table 1.1 lists some of the most common questions.

Table 1.1
What Teachers Ask About the Act

What is the 1981 Education Act?
What is Circular 1/83?
What are the Regulations?

For whom is the Act intended?
Does it affect me?
Don't all children have special needs?

How does it affect me?
Will the Act affect other teachers in my school?
Is teaching pupils with Special Educational Needs now the
   responsibility of all teachers?

What is a Statement?
What is Advice?
What is meant by 'a significantly greater difficulty in learning'?

How does a child get a Statement?
Which children will need a Statement?
How should the Act be implemented?
How do I cope with the extra administration?

What are the implications of the Act with respect to curriculum
   planning, teaching and record keeping?
Will the Act lead to increased accountability?
Will the Act lead to an increase in the number of children with special
   needs integrated into ordinary schools?

How do we assess the children concerned?
What tests do we use to assess their needs?

Table 1.1 continued

Will additional resources be made available?

How does the Act give increased rights to parents?

What is the role of the support services?

These questions reflect a broad range of themes. In particular they relate to:

— the purpose of the Act,

— definitions of specific terms,

— the procedures to be followed when implementing the Act,

— the intended target population,

— how children's needs should be assessed,

— the roles of teachers, parents and the support services,

— implications for teachers in terms of everyday classroom, teaching and administrative responsibilities.

— implications for future resources.

These issues are dealt with thoughout the book as we examine the Act, its terminology and implications for practice. The emphasis throughout is not only on establishing principles for meeting the specific requirements of the Act, but also on principles which apply to a broader range of pupils with special needs. We would go further and express the view that teaching children with 'special needs' *highlights aspects of good practice* which are relevant to all children, not just those who have been reported as experiencing difficulties. Special education is not an adjunct to mainstream education, but an essential component within it; in this sense special needs is a *continuum*, not a category.

The one theme that perhaps receives less attention than others is that of resources. The Act clearly has resource implications which have been widely acknowledged. Unfortunately this has not always led to funds being made available to schools to enable the necessary provision to be made. It is not the intention of this book to examine the political reasons for this, either at a central or local government level, as they are largely beyond the power of individual teachers or schools to influence directly.

What we offer instead is an account of how the Act can be responded to positively in the classroom, given the constraints that typically operate. Whilst taking this approach, we are *not* tacitly assuming that existing resources are adequate to meet current needs or that they should not be subject to frequent review. Indeed, where the possibility exists of securing improvements in resources for special needs we would vigorously endorse efforts to pursue such opportunities at a variety of levels. Whatever our aspirations for the future, we need to bear in mind the realities of the here and now, and the needs of the children currently in school. We hope that readers of this book will gain encouragement in their continuing efforts to develop positive policies and practices to meet special needs in response to the 1981 Education Act.

Chapter Two

TRENDS IN SPECIAL EDUCATION

This chapter looks at the early forms of special education and discusses major changes that have taken place. Six main themes are identified (Table 2.1) in which some of the most significant developments have occurred and which can possibly be seen as signposting areas of debate for the future.

Table 2.1
Themes in Special Education

Concepts of special education
Categories of handicap
Identification and assessment procedures
Integration
Parental involvement
Responsibility of the school

The chapter then considers special education in the social context in which it is practised together with an overview of developments in the field elsewhere in Europe and USA. Finally we conclude with thoughts on what we feel can be learned from what has happened so far.

EARLY FORMS OF SPECIAL EDUCATION

Prior to the establishment of universal ordinary education through the Education Acts passed in the 1870s and 1880s, the first forms of 'special education' appeared in the latter part of the 18th century. The first school for the deaf was operated by the Thomas Braidwood Academy for the Deaf and Dumb and Henry Dannett opened the first school for the blind in Liverpool, a private venture offering vocational training. The mid 19th century saw the first provision for 'mentally defective' children at an asylum for 'idiots' at Highgate. They had previously been confined to the depressing conditions of the Victorian workhouses. Tomlinson (1982) points out that these early forms of special education were often motivated by commercial rather than educational or charitable factors. The aim was frequently to make its recipients useful and productive members of society, usually in an economic sense.

Following the creation of state education, the London School Board in 1874, formed a class for deaf children at a public elementary school, which is often seen as the starting point for 'formal' special education. Early state schools operated a Payment by Results Scheme, teachers' salaries being linked to children's educational achievement. Transfers to special schools therefore may not always have been prompted by a concern for the child's best interests and educational needs.

Between 1900-1944, increasing numbers of children were felt to be in need of an alternative form of education. However, the political influences of the time cannot be readily dismissed and of particular concern was the number of working class children who were placed in special schools. There were a number of reasons for this and a careful analysis of events at the time can provide invaluable insights into the development of special education and its frequently low status within the education system as a whole.

Excellent summaries of the history of special education are to be found in the Warnock Report (DES, 1978, Chapter 2) and Tomlinson (1982) who examine the area in the light of prevailing social, economic and professional concerns. This perspective is especially helpful in putting past and present events in special education into a broader context.

The 1944 Education Act saw an increase from four to eleven, in the number of categories of children requiring special education. Again special education was seen to be something that took place predominantly outside the ordinary school in special schools. A large number of new schools were therefore built to cater for the increased demand, the biggest growth area being the number of children deemed 'educationally subnormal' (ESN), who required their own form of provision. During the 1960s the ESN (Mild) population was by far the largest category of children ascertained as handicapped (64%) (Tomlinson, 1982).

The 1970s saw further significant changes in special education, some of which were to have far-reaching implications. In 1973, a committee under the chairmanship of Mrs Mary Warnock was set up to review the educational provision for handicapped children. Its findings were published in a government report entitled Special Educational Needs (DES, 1978).

Circular 2/75 (The Discovery of Children Requiring Special Education and the Assessment of Their Needs) represented an attempt to look at children's educational needs and not just to identify the nature of a pupil's handicap. This is encapsulated in the now defunct, 'special education' (SE) forms 1-3, which were to be used when placing children in special schools.

Finally, in 1976, section 10 of the Education Act specified that children should only be placed in special schools if they could not be given efficient instruction within mainstream education, or if such instruction would cause 'unreasonable public expenditure'. Although this section was never implemented, for economic reasons, it offered encouragement to those who believed an increasing number of children, who were being segregated and placed in special schools, could, given adequate resources, be taught in their neighbourhood, mainstream school.

Table 2.2 outlines some major events and important government legislation relating to special education since 1900.

Table 2.2
Some Important Developments in Special Education

1908	Royal Commission on care and control of the 'feeble-minded' reported, stating that institutional provision for mentally defective children on occupational lines was preferable to provision in special schools — responsibility should lie with local mental deficiency committees.
1913	Mental Deficiency Act required LEAs to ascertain and certify which children aged between seven and 16 were defective.
1913	Cyril Burt appointed by London County Council Education Department as the country's first school psychologist.
1914	Elementary Education (Defective and Epileptic Children) Act required LEAs to make provision for mentally defective children.
1921	Education Act enabled local authorities to compel parents of 'certified' children to send them to special schools.
1926	A special Children's Department established within the Tavistock Clinic.
1927	East London Child Guidance Clinic set up.
1929	Mental Deficiency Committee concluded that of the total number of 'mentally defective' children; only one third had been ascertained and only one half of these were attending special schools; a further 10% of all children were retarded and failing to make progress in ordinary schools.
1931	First LEA School Psychological Service (Leicester).
1932	First LEA Child Guidance Clinic (Birmingham).
1944	Education Act required LEAs to provide education for children according to age, ability and aptitude. Under Section 34, each LEA had the duty of ascertaining children from 'a disability of body or mind' and to provide 'special educational treatment' in special schools or elsewhere.
1945	Handicapped Pupils and Health Service Regulations defined 11 categories of handicap which were modified to ten in 1953.
1955	Since the 1944 Act the number of children in special schools had risen, from 38 499 to 58 034 (an increase of 57%) and the number of schools from 528 to 743 (an increase of 40%).

Table 2.2 continued

1959	The Mental Health Act gave parents extra time to appeal against the LEA's decision that a child was incapable of being educated at school, and the right to a review after one year.
1970	Under the Education Act, LEAs assumed responsibility for mentally handicapped children who had previously been placed under the care of Health Authorities.
1973	Warnock Committee set up to consider the education of handicapped children and young people.
1975	DES Circular 2/75 considered the *'Discovery of Children Requiring Special Education and the Assessment of Their Needs'*.
1976	Section 10 of the Education Act placed responsibility on LEAs to provide special education in ordinary schools when practicable.
1978	The Warnock Committee published its findings *(Special Educational Needs)*.
1979	180 000 children in state special schools.
1981	Education Act 1981 received Royal Assent.
1983	Education Act 1981 came into force on 1st April.

Underlying these developments have been a number of discernible trends, which due to the course they have taken, help explain why so much was expected of the 1981 Education Act. These trends represent significant shifts in attitudes towards children with special needs.

THEMES IN SPECIAL EDUCATION

Concepts of Special Education

From the inception of special education children who have received it have always been seen as different from the norm. The first special schools were for the deaf and blind, later ones catering for 'mental defectives'. These children were regarded as having something wrong with them. They lacked either the mental or physical (and sometimes both) attributes of other children and were thus regarded as handicapped in some way. It was the child who had the deficiency and therefore the problem, and this was dealt with by segregating them from their 'normal' peers.

Children were thought of entirely in terms of their handicap, and it was invariably assumed that all those children having a particular handicapping condition, comprised a homogeneous group. All blind children were therefore grouped together and placed in the same type of school as were the deaf, physically handicapped etc. Classification of children in this way gave little consideration to other significant aspects of their development.

Inevitably, with the emergence of extensive segregated education after the 1944 Education Act, these assumptions have increasingly been questioned. Pupils vary considerably in the extent to which their actual levels of performance in school-related activities are affected by their handicap. Even though children have the same handicap, their actual educational needs may differ.

Wedell (1973) has emphasised how children are able to compensate to different degrees for the handicaps they experience. They utilise other skills and strengths and, in many instances, are able to overcome what at one time may have been viewed as considerable problems. A view gathering momentum at this time was that the way in which a child with a handicap interacted with her environment was as important, if not more so, then the specific nature of the diagnosed condition.

Those involved in special education became increasingly aware of the necessity to look at children in broader terms. It was no longer sufficient to be given a medical diagnosis of what was 'wrong' with a child. Of far greater significance was finding out what skills children had already learned and what they needed to be taught next. How did they interact with peers and their environment in general? What strengths did they have to help them overcome their difficulties?

Now, when thinking of which children might require some form of special educational provision, the questions to be answered are not simply, 'What is wrong with the child?' or 'How is he handicapped?' but 'What are the child's educational needs?' and 'What would be the most suitable provision to meet those needs?' The crucial shift in emphasis has been from *categories of handicap* to *specification of educational needs*. This essential distinction between analysis of the difficulty, identifying needs and specifying provision was made clear in DES Circular 1/83 (see Chapter 4).

Categories of Handicap and Terminology

Looking back at earlier categories of handicap is a salutory experience, serving to remind us how far things have progressed within a relatively short period. It also signposts the inherent dangers of labels and descriptions of children based solely on their handicaps. Statutory categories of handicap between 1886–1981 are shown in Table 2.3.

A quick glance at Table 2.3 indicates that although we may no longer categorise children in terms of whether they are 'idiots' or 'imbeciles' or 'mental defectives', the labels have survived in common usage. It is interesting to observe that to an individual they convey only *negative connotations*. They are included and defined in the Concise Oxford Dictionary but without reference to their earlier legal standing.

Other terms are clearly more closely related to a specific medical condition, for example epilepsy, but we do not think of those suffering from epilepsy or diabetes in quite the same way as implied in the 11 categories of handicap emerging from the 1944 Education Act.

Table 2.3
Statutory Categories of Handicap 1886–1981 (Tomlinson, 1982)

| Statutory categories | | | | | | Suggested descriptive categories |
1886	1899	1913	1945	1962	1970	1981
Idiot	Idiot	Idiot	Severely subnormal (SSN)	Severely subnormal (SSN)	Educationally subnormal (severe)	Child with learning difficulties (severe)
Imbecile	Imbecile	Imbecile				
		Moral imbecile		Psychopathic		
	Blind	Blind	Blind		Blind	Blind
			Partially sighted		Partially sighted	Partially sighted
	Deaf	Deaf	Deaf		Deaf	Deaf
			Partially deaf	Partial hearing	Partial hearing	Partial hearing
	Epileptic	Epileptic	Epileptic		Epileptic	Epileptic
	Defective	Mental defective (feeble-minded)	Educationally subnormal		Educationally subnormal (mild or moderate)	Child with learning difficulty (mild or moderate)
			Maladjusted		Maladjusted	Maladjusted disruptive
		Physical defective	Physically handicapped		Physically handicapped	Physically handicapped
			Speech defect		Speech defect	Speech defect
			Delicate	Delicate	Delicate	Delicate
			Diabetic			
						Dyslexic? Autistic?

Special educational needs

Note. Categories suggested but never adopted include: the neuropathic child, the inconsequential child, the psychiatrically crippled child, the aphasic child and others. Autism and dyslexia were recognised under the 1970 Chronically Sick and Disabled Persons Act.

The 1981 Education Act gives LEAs the responsibility for identifying and making appropriate provision for all those children with special educational needs. No reference is made in the relevant documents to types of handicap. These have now been superseded by the more general but more humane and useful concept of special educational need.

Identification and Assessment Procedures

The most commonly used assessment device in special education in recent times, has been the intelligence test. This has its origins in the mental testing movement reflected in the work of Charles Spearman and Cyril Burt in the UK, Alfred Binet in France in the early part of the century and later David Wechsler in the USA. The major intention of such workers was to devise measures that would predict future academic performance.

The main argument in favour of the use of these instruments would run broadly as follows. The assumption was made that children differed in their levels of intelligence and this was directly associated with their potential to learn. Those with higher levels of intelligence were therefore considered as being capable of learning more and learning more quickly, than their less well endowed counterparts. When children experienced educational difficulties, it was thought learning potential could be estimated through the use of such measures and the resulting intelligence quotient (IQ).

Intelligence tests were therefore used to distinguish between two groups of children experiencing difficulties. On the one hand were the children who, although behind their peers in acquiring basic literacy and numeracy skills, were thought on the basis of their IQ scores to be capable of benefitting from extra help *within* the ordinary school. They would be the children who would comprise the 'remedial' group and receive assistance usually on a withdrawal basis, from the school's remedial teacher or department.

A second group of children, scoring much lower on the IQ test (traditionally IQ 70 or below) were considered to be less suited to ordinary school provision and so would be recommended for transfer to special school. They were termed 'backward' or 'retarded' rather than remedial and would need resources and teaching approaches not readily available within the mainstream sector.

It is important to recognise that this line of thought is based on a number of assumptions, namely:
— that intelligence has a *causal* and not merely correlational relationship with academic performance,
— that an IQ score provides a reliable estimate of intelligence,
— that measured IQs represent a largely fixed level of intelligence,
— that IQs are accurate predictors of future scholastic achievement.
The discussion and debate surrounding the nature and measurement of

intelligence has been going on for a long time and is still one of education's 'hot potatoes'. However, what can be said is that the above assumptions have been increasingly called into question (for example Engelmann, 1970; Kamin, 1974; Gillie, 1978; Simon, 1978, 1985; Beloff, 1980; Eysenck and Kamin, 1981).

There is another aspect of the mental testing approach used to find out what was wrong with the child. A range of tests would often have been given by educational psychologists, remedial advisory teachers, doctors, speech therapists, etc., all designed to determine the cause of the difficulty and why progress was not being made. The assessment could be seen as a process which rarely produced specific implications for future teaching, for example what needed to be taught next and how best to teach.

This type of assessment was also characterised by being carried out on a single occasion only, with decisions about a child's educational future being based on how the child performed in that situation. Furthermore, the assessment was rarely completed in the environment most familiar and comfortable to the child, his own classroom. The pupil would usually be removed and taken either elsewhere in the school (often the medical room) or have to go to a different place altogether, maybe a Child Guidance Centre, Health Centre or hospital. It would be asking a lot of a pupil, already aware and sensitive that he was experiencing difficulties in school, to perform at an optimal level, in a strange environment with an unfamiliar person, quite apart from the crucial problem of generalising the findings obtained in this situation to the typical classroom setting.

The assessment was not curriculum related, that is to say, the focus of attention was not directly on the area of classroom learning in which the child was experiencing difficulties. Instead the assessment frequently aimed to identify *deficits* in hypothesised 'underlying' abilities. Evidence for the validity of this is now being seriously questioned. This sort of assessment placed an undue emphasis on what may be called *within-child variables* and in doing so, did not take sufficient account of the *interaction* between pupil, teacher and curriculum (see Figure 2.1).

Associated with IQ and other forms of testing were the various role expectations of the different participants. Teachers identified the pupils who were having difficulties in school, expressed concern to the appropriate outside agency, which was subsequently invited to provide answers as to why the child's progress was not satisfactory.

This classically places the member of the outside agency in the role of 'expert' with the teacher cast as the 'non-expert' consumer. This fails to recognise the equally valid expertise of both parties and has on occasions led to considerable dissatisfaction, and professional mistrust.

Over recent years the concept of assessment has changed. Assessment is now more appropriately seen as an on-going process which is curriculum related and school based. Outside agencies are increasingly

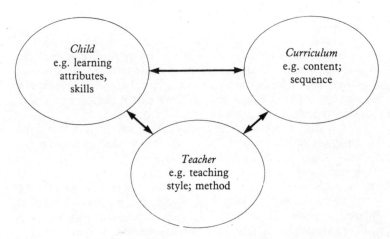

Figure 2.1 The interactive nature of learning.

working in collaboration with teachers, offering an alternative area of knowledge, skills and expertise, which is complementary to that of the teacher rather than superior to it. Indeed the whole assessment process has gradually come to be seen as a partnership between different professions. These emerging trends have been encapsulated in the principles underlying the Education Act and its accompanying Circular 1/83, and we shall be discussing their practical implications in more detail in Chapters 5 and 6.

Integration

The IQ test was the main device that oiled the wheels of segregated education. It was presented as being a valid 'scientific' instrument which could measure innate potential and predict future academic performance. As the validity of IQ testing became increasingly questioned so did the practice of segregated special education.

IQ tests were not only used predictively within special education. They were also adopted as part of the Eleven Plus examinations which evolved out of the 1944 Education Act. But while the problems of accurately predicting future performance at the age of 11 were debated extensively, eventually resulting in the wide-scale abandonment of the procedure, and the creation of comprehensive education, there was no equivalent action taken in relation to selection for special schools.

However, integration has now emerged as a major issue, with persuasive moral, political and educational arguments being advanced for the increased integration into mainstream education of children with special educational needs.

Parental Involvement

The role and rights of parents has changed during the evolution of special education. Probably as a result of the medical nature of the initial procedures for designating children as handicapped, parents were usually in the position of having to accept special school placement as a *fait accompli*. It would have been a brave parent indeed who would challenge the expressed views of the LEA's experts.

As the trends in assessment have changed, so has the involvement of parents in the new procedures. In the past they would be notified of the different stages of the referral and assessment process but their involvement was rarely active and largely confined to a view from the touchline. Assessment procedures have been developed which have necessitated a closer working relationship and partnership between different professionals, which has also been extended to parents. Their active participation, collaboration and involvement is keenly sought. Their rights, as parents, are respected and their understanding and perceptions of their children increasingly recognised and valued.

There are also a larger number of voluntary advisory bodies available to offer independent advice to parents. For example, in relation to the 1981 Education Act, the Advisory Centre for Education (ACE) has produced a series of informative booklets, summarising and highlighting their rights within the new legislative procedures.

The last five years has also seen the development of a number of imaginative 'parents as teachers' projects (for example, Topping and Wolfendale, 1985 and Topping, 1986). These have focused on showing parents how to help their children learn the skills with which they have been having difficulties at school. These schemes have developed from the recognition that parents and teachers can collectively harness their respective resources and expertise, in an effective partnership which ultimately has considerable benefits for the children involved.

The Responsibility of the School

Initially, the main role of the school was to inform the appropriate LEA personnel and advisory agencies that a child was having difficulties and was probably in need of a placement in a special school. The school took little part in the assessment and subsequent decision-making over the most suitable form of provision.

The 1944 Education Act and then 30 years later, DES Circular 2/75 required the school to play a larger role. The headteacher would be asked for his or her views about the child's academic progress, behaviour, social relationships, etc. and to suggest the provision most likely to meet the child's needs. The nature of the comments made was, however, essentially retrospective and summative. Schools were still not integrally involved in the assessment procedure which was seen to be operated predominantly by the medical officers and educational psychologists. As a result, it is extremely likely that many teachers felt that their contribution to the process carried less weight than that of the other professionals involved.

The 1981 Education Act places a much greater responsibility on schools, than they have previously experienced, to identify, assess and make recommendations about provision for children with special needs. Now, the new assessment procedure places them in a *central* role and grants them parity with the other professionals involved.

SPECIAL EDUCATION AND ITS SOCIAL CONTEXT

When looking at trends and specific events in special education, the temptation is to focus on what has happened and take it out of the social and political context in which it occurred. To do so can convey a distorted view of the development of special education.

We have alluded to the fact that not everything in special education has arisen from altruistic motives. The first special schools were set up as businesses. Segregated state education was, in part, determined by the Payment by Results Scheme, leading to teachers wanting to remove troublesome elements from their midst. Even integration, which is widely advocated, could be viewed negatively as a cost-cutting, money-saving exercise. Falling rolls have meant smaller classes in all sectors of the education system. Integration would allow mainstream schools to increase their numbers, special schools could be closed and money could be saved by not having to pay special school teachers their special education supplement. It is not the purpose of this book to provide a sociological and political analysis of the 1981 Education Act. However, we feel it is important to bear in mind its origins and the economic and political climate surrounding its implementation. This is equally true when looking at the historical developments and in this context Tomlinson (1982) proves a good source of reference.

SPECIAL EDUCATION AROUND THE WORLD

The trends in special education identified in this chapter have also been recognised internationally and in several instances legislative backing has appeared to support these developments. In particular, Public Law 94–142, in the United States of America in 1975, made school boards responsible for ensuring children with special needs be educated in 'the least restrictive environment', a phrase essentially encouraging integration.

Elsewhere in Europe governments have passed Acts of Parliament to safeguard the rights of those with special needs and to ensure that appropriate provision is made for them. These changes were represented in the Sundberg Declaration which was drawn up in 1981 during the UNESCO Conference held in Spain. It makes reference to the basic right of all handicapped people to education, training, cultural activities and information, and suggests measures to be taken to reduce the handicapping effects of disabilities and maximise integration in society (Fish, 1985).

WHAT WE HAVE LEARNED

The 1981 Education Act is the latest in a long line of government legislation relating to children with special needs and it reflects the progress that has been achieved in a relatively short period of time. The emerging trends have all helped set the scene for developing positive responses to the difficulties children experience in schools.

In recent years much of what has been written about special education has encouraged:

— increased parental involvement;

— steps towards increasing levels of integration;

— a desire to identify children's needs and not merely categorise handicaps;

— moves towards continuous assessment procedures which are based on classroom activities and children's experiences in school.

Our interpretation of the Act has inevitably been influenced by the lessons that have already been learned in teaching children with special needs. Whilst we can readily acknowledge and welcome the advances that have been made, we would also recognise a danger of slipping back into old ways after the initial impact of a new piece of legislation has subsided.

This book is being written at a time when there are many hotly disputed issues confronting those who work in LEAs. As these issues receive prominence, the 1981 Education Act may fade from the front line of everyday thinking. A look at last week's newspapers serves as a sharp reminder of how short lived one day's news can be. So it can be with educational issues. Whilst those whose lives are affected daily have a constant reminder of current concerns, others whose contact is less frequent, may have more difficulty in keeping abreast of new developments.

Labelling

One danger that is generally appreciated is the effects of labelling. We have traced the development of earlier terminology and can only hope 'special needs' does not attract the negative connotations of previous labels. Certainly, at the moment, the term 'special needs' sounds more humane than some of its predecessors but there was a time when 'slow learner' was preferable to 'backward'. Each new label seems to have an active life of several years before being replaced by one that is more in keeping with current educational acceptability.

Without doubt, we are just at one point on a *continuum* and there is always a danger that the phrase 'children with special needs' will ossify, with all pupils thus labelled being thought of as one homogeneous group of handicapped children. The label may then have the same negative status of its precursors.

Observing changes in terminology can be a bit like watching a Peter Sellers film and trying to spot him when he appears disguised as different characters. The disguise is often effective but underneath it is usually possible to detect our old friend. There is always the concern that adopting the term 'special needs' will also be cosmetic and not promote more fundamental changes.

The purpose of the term 'special needs' is to direct attention to a pupil's needs: to ask what it is she needs to be taught and what provision will help to meet those needs. This response brings thinking in line with how we might consider the educational needs of *all* children in a class. The legislation thus encourages teachers to perceive those pupils experiencing difficulties and their needs in the same way as their peers. It is not necessary to ask a different set of questions when a particular child is not learning as well as might be expected. They are the same questions that would be posed when deciding how best to teach any child.

Teacher Expectations

By looking at *all* children in similar ways it is possible that the negative effects of teacher expectations on pupil performance can be mitigated. This is again another well documented area (Barker-Lunn, 1970; Elashoff and Snow, 1971; Insel and Jacobson, 1975; Burns, 1982). It is now recognised that how well children perform at school can be strongly influenced by the expectations teachers have of them. Clearly, through having notions of pupils being 'handicapped', our expectations of their future performance are likely to be lower than if they were perceived as 'non-handicapped'. When looking at children in a class, and generally asking of all of them: 'What are their educational needs?', it might be easier to steer clear of having lower expectations of some children than others.

In recent years there have been a number of approaches introduced in the field of special education which have served as poignant reminders of this point. The results of Project Follow Through in the USA (Becker, 1977; Becker *et al.*, 1981) illustrated how the progress of children experiencing difficulties could be accelerated in learning early numeracy and literacy skills. The effects of Conductive Education on teaching children with cerebral palsy, pioneered at the Peto Institute in Budapest, have created widespread interest in the UK (Cottam and Sutton, 1986). Children in the past who may have remained bound to a wheelchair for life have exceeded previous expectations and in some cases are now able to walk and are progressing towards leading independent and fulfilling lives. They will have opportunities to lead life in a way hitherto rarely considered.

Similarly Instrumental Enrichment is an approach that is prompting many of those working in the field of special education to reappraise their current thinking about the 'learning potential' of children experiencing difficulties (Sharron, 1987). Instrumental Enrichment incorporates teaching stategies that enable pupils to learn cognitive operations at a level once considered beyond their reach.

Much of this work, although new and currently the subject of field research in the UK, is leading to a drastic *reappraisal* of previous expectations about what children perceived to have difficulties can achieve in school. Frank Smith (1978) points out in his article 'The Politics of Ignorance', that before children start school, 'they have already resolved intellectual problems of astounding complexity — should we pause to think about it — ranging from mastering a language to organising coherent theory of the world around them, including their own place on it'. If they have achieved this, should we not also expect that they should learn, in Smith's view, the less complex skill of reading?

It appears that we are nowhere near reaching an understanding of what children are capable of learning. However, what can be asserted with some confidence, is that our expectations can often be an extremely influential factor in determining what children can achieve in schools.

Flexibility

Teaching is a dynamic process within which the needs of children may change at regular intervals. In the newspapers, recently published books and staff room discussions, it is often said that *all children have special educational needs*. Given the way children are now designated as having special needs, this statement cannot be considered accurate, in the strict terms of the 1981 Act (see Cox, 1985). However, it is unquestionable that *all children have educational needs*, and will require differing levels of teacher time and attention during their school careers. On occasions, some children will need more direct contact, planning and administrative time from their teachers than others.

At various times, a range of pupils might be thought to have needs which require 'special' arrangements to be made for them. It is important to remember that it may not always be necessary to organise such provision. Similarly, if we are tempted to think of some children's educational needs as being 'special' it is surely preferable to recognise that such an epithet is used flexibly and is not immutable.

Being a 'Good Enough' Teacher

An obvious concern of those working within the field of special education is the level of funding available to implement the Act. Within

LEAs, administrators and advisers will allocate varying sums of money and resources to schools to help teach children experiencing difficulties. Certainly those within the LEA hierarchy specifically, and central government generally, can make life easier in some respects, but ultimately headteachers and teachers have to do the teaching with the resources currently at their disposal. In one view, it will be *the teacher's own feelings of competence, optimism and well-being that are key contributory factors in determining the success of children's learning.*

To accept the responsibility for what happens in a classroom does not automatically imply an acceptance of existing LEA provision. It is still valid to make appropriate representations to the relevant personnel for improving provision.

However, whilst accepting responsibility, it is also important to acknowledge that only so much can be achieved with current resources. In other words, a teacher has, in our view, to be willing to assert that he or she is doing as much as is feasible within existing circumstances and to be satisfied with being 'good enough'. It is inevitable that teachers will always feel the regret of *if only* ... more funding were available, better resources provided, smaller classes, additional specialist advice, etc. Nevertheless, the fact remains that every teacher is obliged to make the best of what is *currently* available, and derive satisfaction from doing whatever they can under existing circumstances.

Focus on Factors which can be Influenced

This leads to a final point. There is a range of factors over which teachers have some direct influence in schools and others which fall outside this range. We have already referred to some of these 'external' factors and will elaborate on others in the chapters on assessment. Among the factors within the teacher's control are the teacher's theoretical knowledge, enthusiasm, skills at managing the classroom environment and children's learning experiences and the general organisation of special education provision within the school. These are all, at times, subject to external constraints but can nevertheless be harnessed towards making a significant, positive contribution to meeting children's educational needs.

The lessons learned from the past should serve as a springboard for future action. Perhaps the most important lesson we should bear in mind is that the field of special education is always changing. What is described in this book is the latest in the line of government legislation. It is unlikely to be the last.

FURTHER READING

Barton, L. and Tomlinson, S. eds (1981). *Special Education: Policy, Practices and Social Issues*, Harper and Row, London.

This book investigates what special education is, why a system of special education has developed and what actually goes on in special schools.

Barton, L. and Tomlinson, S. eds (1984). *Special Education and Social Interests*, Croom Helm, London.

Considers the broad social context for special education, including international comparisons, especially developments in North America.

Tomlinson, S. (1982). *A Sociology of Special Education*, Routledge and Kegan Paul, London.

An excellent source book providing a coherent sociological perspective on special education.

Weddell, K. ed (1975). *Orientations in Special Education*, Wiley, London.

A book of reading which considers recent assumptions and concepts in special education.

Chapter Three

WHAT DOES THE 1981 EDUCATION ACT SAY?

In this chapter we will clarify the nature and purpose of the documents that relate to the 1981 Education Act and then summarise the main issues which apply to mainstream schools. The Act has generated a considerable amount of paper and clearly not everyone will have the time to go to source and read all the available materials. We will therefore highlight and look at the main themes emerging from the Act in a constructive way, particularly in relation to its implications for teachers and schools.

The basic documents connected with the Act are as follows:
— Circular 8/81: Education Act 1981,
— Education Act 1981,
— The Education (Special Educational Needs) Regulations 1983,
— Circular 1/83: Assessments and Statements of Special Educational Needs.

The Education Act 1981 and the Education Regulations 1983 comprise the new law on special education. They contain the provisions which are now the legal requirements for each LEA in England and Wales to uphold.

The Circulars (8/81 and 1/83) have quite different implications for LEAs. A footnote on each Circular emphasises their legal status: 'A Circular cannot be regarded as providing an authoritative legal interpretation of any of the provisions of the Act as this is exclusively a function of the Courts'. These Circulars do not carry mandatory requirements but convey something of the current 'spirit' of special education, with its attendant perceptions of how to view the nature of the child's difficulties, the assessment process, identification of a pupil's special educational needs and decisions about making appropriate provision to meet those needs.

Circular 8/81 appeared before the Act was implemented and was intended to give LEAs advance notification of the main provisions and implications of the Act. The more significant document, 1/83 appeared shortly before the Act was implemented. This Circular considers the implications of the Act and accompanying regulations for the assessment of a broad range of special educational needs. It provides guidelines for LEAs in implementing the new Statutory Assessment procedure. We will look at the recommendations of this Circular in more detail in Chapter 4.

Our intention in this chapter is to clarify the main provisions of the Act and the Education Regulations. We draw out key themes and issues but do not propose to do a fine-grained legal analysis.

The Act itself is divided into 21 separate sections covering:
— definitions of 'special educational needs' and 'special educational provision',
— identification and assessment of children with special educational needs,
— special schools and approved independent schools,
— school attendance orders.

We do not intend to cover all the sections of the Act but will concentrate on those areas which are most relevant for mainstream schools (Sections 1, 2, 4, 5, 7–9) and will summarise the significant points of the omitted sections. Other summaries of the Act have been produced by the Advisory Centre for Education (ACE; Newell, 1983 written especially for parents) and by the National Union of Teachers. A detailed legal analysis of the Education Act has been carried out by Cox (1985) in a book entitled *The Law of Special Educational Needs*.

SECTION 1   DEFINITIONS WITHIN THE ACT

The opening section defines three terms: *special educational needs, learning difficulty* and *special educational provision.*

A child has *'special educational needs* if he has a learning difficulty which calls for special educational provision to be made for him'

Subsection 1(1)

A child has a *learning difficulty* if,
(a) he has a significantly greater difficulty in learning than the majority of children of his age; or
(b) he has a disability which either prevents or hinders him from making use of educational facilities of a kind generally provided in schools, within the area of the local authority concerned, for children of his age; or
(c) he is under the age of five years and is, or would be if special educational provision were not made for him, likely to fall within paragraph (a) or (b) when over that age.

Subsection 2

Special educational provision means
(a) in relation to a child who has attained the age of two years, educational provision which is additional to, or otherwise different from, the educational provision made generally for

> children of his age in schools maintained by the local education
> authority concerned; and
> (b) in relation to any child under that age, educational provision
> of any kind.
>
> **Subsection 3**

A pupil is therefore seen to have a special educational need if he has a
learning difficulty which requires special educational provision. The
Act thus establishes that a special educational need only exists when
special educational provision is made. Within the terms of reference of
the Act, a child cannot have a special educational need without special
educational provision being made available. (This link between need
and provision becomes ambiguous in the context of Circular 1/83. It
stresses that identification of needs should be made without reference to
available provision. This apparent contradiction will be discussed in
Chapter 4.)

Whether such provision is made will clearly depend on the policy and
existing provision within the LEA. As LEAs differ in the forms of
provision currently available to meet children's needs, it would seem
that there will be differences among LEAs in identifying which
children are recognised as having special educational needs.

The situation could arise whereby two children with similar
educational needs, in neighbouring authorities, receive different
treatment under the Act. One may be deemed to have 'special
educational needs' because *additional provision* has to be made available
within the LEA to meet his educational needs. Therefore by offering:

> educational provision which is additional to, or otherwise
> different from, the educational provision made generally for
> children of his age in schools maintained by the LEA,
>
> **Subsection 3 (a)**

the child's educational needs are 'special'.

The second child however, may already be receiving the required
provision, within the context of his present school. Presumably he
would not be considered as having 'special educational needs' since his
needs were currently being met without the necessity of additional
provision.

As a result, the question of whether a child has special educational
needs is determined by the appropriateness and suitability of *existing
provision*. It is not, as might have been expected, related directly to a
child's specific educational needs, considered in isolation, without
reference to existing resources and their deployment.

This definition, as well as causing *discrepancies* between LEAs could
also create problems *within* an authority. Schools inevitably do not

employ their finances and teaching resources in the same way. The general needs of the children and the catchment area will in part determine how resources are distributed within a school. Consequently a situation could arise in an authority where children with similar needs could be treated differently under the terms of the Act.

The definition of whether a child has a learning difficulty also creates a number of problems of interpretation. The first concerns the phrase:

> **significantly greater difficulty in learning**
> **Subsection 2(a)**

By what criteria can one child's difficulty in learning be considered 'significantly greater' than another's? In one sense, to talk about 'significant difference' is to borrow statistical terminology and apply it to education. This can create the impression that the extent of a child's difficulty in learning is:

— quantifiable,
— measurable,
— of such a nature that it can be compared with that of another
— and that differences emerging following such comparisons can ultimately be expressed in terms of a statistical significance.

This is an issue which we will return to and discuss in Chapter 4. However, it is worth remembering that one of the emerging trends in special education, which is also reflected in the recommendations to LEAs incorporated into Circular 1/83, is a move away from forms of assessment based solely on the use of norm referenced psychometric test results. In practice, it seems most likely that judgements about the extent of a child's difficulty in learning will be a *subjective* matter, based on detailed knowledge of the child, local circumstances and LEA provision. It would be misleading to think these decisions could be determined simply by reliance on measurable and statistically significant differences between children's attainments.

A second area of concern relates to the phrase:

> **the majority of children of his age**
> **Subsection 2(a)**

It is unclear which peer group the child in question should be compared with. Is it the children in his class, school, catchment area, LEA, area of the country, etc.? The larger the comparison group, the more difficult it will be to get reliable information on which to base decision-making. This would also increase the likelihood of comparisons being made on the most easily collected and accessible information, which would be the results of a child's performance on standardised tests of ability and attainment.

Where the peer group comparisons are restricted to children within the immediate locality, either the school or catchment area, the information used is likely to be more reliable, valid and related to local circumstances. Resulting decisions will subsequently be better informed and based on a more thorough understanding of the salient factors affecting a child's future education and most appropriate forms of provision.

Finally, it is important to note that a caveat is added in Subsection 4, relating to children whose first language is other than English:

> **a child is not to be taken as having a learning difficulty solely because the language (or form of the language) in which he is, or will be, taught is different from a language (or form of language) which has at any time been spoken in his home.**
>
> **Subsection 4**

As a result, those children for whom English is a second language are excluded from the provisions of the Act, where it is felt that language alone is the main contributory factor in their experiencing a difficulty in learning.

SECTION 2 · PROVISION OF SPECIAL EDUCATION

It is now the duty of LEAs to ensure that special educational provision is made for pupils who have special educational needs. Furthermore as long as a number of conditions are met, where special educational provision is made for a child for whom they maintain a Statement (see discussion under Section 7 of this chapter and Chapters 4 and 6 for an explanation of this term), it is the duty of the LEA to secure that he is educated in an ordinary school.

The conditions which need to be satisfied are as follows:

> **that account has been taken, in accordance with Section 7, of the views of the child's parent and that educating the child in the ordinary school is compatible with**
> **(a) his receiving the special educational provision that he requires;**
> **(b) the provision of efficient education for the children with whom he will be educated; and**
> **(c) the efficient use of resources.**
>
> **Subsection 3**

Furthermore:

> **Where a child who has special educational needs is being educated in an ordinary school maintained by a local education authority it shall be the duty of those concerned with making**

special educational provision for the child to secure, so far as is both compatible with the objectives mentioned in paragraphs (a) to (c) of Subsection (3) above and reasonably practicable, that the child engages in the activities of the school together with children who do not have special educational needs.

Subsection 7

The Act for the first time in the history of education places a duty on LEAs to educate children with special educational needs in the ordinary school subject to the above conditions. When this move is placed in the context of the developments of special education, it is possible to see just how much progress has been made in a relatively short period of time.

However, the conditions which need to be met before integration can go ahead could give the appearance of 'taking back with the one hand what has been given with the other'. It will inevitably be a highly subjective judgement as to whether educating a child with special needs is compatible with the efficient education of his peers and the efficient use of resources. Nevertheless, this should not detract from the significance of enshrining through legislation, the principle of integration. As Cox (1985) states, it is to be hoped that LEAs will interpret the Act with this principle in mind.

A second area covered by Section 2 is the duty placed on school governors to secure that provision is made. It is the duty of governors, in the case of a county or voluntary school, and of the LEA by whom the school is maintained, in the case of maintained nursery school:

(a) to use their best endeavours, in exercising their functions in relation to the school, to secure that if any registered pupil has special educational needs the special educational provision that is required for him is made;
(b) to secure that, where the responsible person has been informed by the LEA that a registered pupil has special educational needs, those needs are made known to all who are likely to teach him; and
(c) to secure that the teachers in the school are aware of the importance of identifying, and providing for, those registered pupils who have special educational needs.

Subsection 5

'Responsible person' means in the case of a county or voluntary school, the headteacher or the appropriate governor, and in the case of a nursery school, the headteacher.

Subsection 6

Except in the case of maintained nursery schools, it is the duty of the governors, rather than the LEA to ensure that special educational provision is made for the individual child. However, this responsibility is also clouded by ambiguity since the governors are only required to deploy their 'best endeavours' which in Cox's eyes (1985) is seen to mean 'best endeavours within the financial resources available' (p. 27), since the government stated when implementing the Act, that it would have no resource implications.

The Act also states that schools should nominate a member of staff, via the headteacher or a governor, to take overall responsibility for children with special needs and many LEAs have now begun to implement this policy. It is further intended that all staff coming into contact with a pupil who has been registered as having special educational needs are made aware of those needs and the necessity of providing for them.

SECTION 4   GENERAL DUTY OF THE LEA TOWARDS CHILDREN FOR WHOM THEY ARE RESPONSIBLE

The Act states:

> **It shall be the duty of every LEA to exercise their powers under this Act with a view to securing that, of the children for whom they are responsible, those with special educational needs which call for the LEA to determine the special educational provision that should be made for them, are identified by the authority.**
> **Subsection 1**

The only children for whom the LEA has to determine the special educational provision are those for whom a Statement is maintained in accordance with Section 7 of the Act. The category of children referred to here therefore are those with disabilities that the Warnock Committee viewed to be complex and long-term and would include approximately 2% of the country's school population.

SECTION 5   ASSESSMENT OF SPECIAL EDUCATIONAL NEEDS

This section requires the LEA to make an assessment of a child's educational needs when they are of the opinion:

> **(a) that he has special educational needs which call for the authority to determine the special educational provision that should be made for him; or**
> **(b) that he probably has such special educational needs.**
> **Subsection 1**

Again, this section of the Act is referring to the smaller group of children who will generally have their educational provision determined by the LEA, and maintained by a Statement (see Section 7).

When the LEA propose to make an assessment under Section 5, they are first of all obliged to inform the child's parents:

> (a) that they propose to make an assessment;
> (b) of the procedure to be followed in making it;
> (c) of the name of the officer of the authority from whom further information may be obtained; and
> (d) of his right to make representations, and submit written evidence, to the authority within such period (which shall not be less than 29 days beginning with the date on which the notice is served) as may be specified in the notice.
>
> Subsection 3

Once the parents have been told of the above, the authority can, after taking into account the parents' views, proceed to assess the child's educational needs. When this course of action is followed, the parents must be duly informed by the LEA.

Once the authority decides to proceed with a formal assessment under this section of the Act, advice is sought from three and sometimes four sources, depending on individual circumstances:
— educational advice,
— medical advice,
— psychological advice,
— any other advice which the authority consider desirable in the case in question for the purpose of arriving at a satisfactory assessment.

The key professionals involved in contributing to an overall assessment of the child's needs are therefore, teachers, medical officers and educational psychologists. The Act gives parity to teachers in terms of their contribution to the assessment process with doctors and psychologists who had hitherto shared the major responsibilities for assessing children's learning difficulties.

The advice offered to the authority by each professional should relate to:
— the educational, medical, psychological or other features of the case (according to the nature of the advice sought) which appear to be relevant to the child's educational needs (including his likely future needs);
— how those features could affect the child's educational needs; and
— the necessary provision to meet those needs, whether by way of special educational provision or non-educational provision.

The school therefore needs to be in a position to comment authoritatively on a child's special educational needs and have views on the most suitable form of provision to meet those needs. The regulations indicate that advice will be requested from the headteacher of the school the child has attended within the preceding 18 months. However, if the pupil has not been at school for this period of time, the authority may seek advice from alternative sources.

If the child has been in attendance at the school for the necessary period, but the headteacher has not taught the child personally within the previous 18 months, the advice should then only be submitted after prior consultation with a teacher who has taught the child. The same circumstances apply when preparing advice on a pupil who is deaf, partially hearing, blind or otherwise visually handicapped. If advice is required with respect to those children, consultations should take place with a person qualified to teach pupils falling into these categories.

All the advice from teachers, medical officers and educational psychologists, after being submitted to the LEA, is made available to the parents when they are sent a copy of the draft statement. All the professionals involved are made responsible for their own independent views. It is a time when a school staff can demonstrate their expertise in describing children's needs, trying to meet them and keeping on-going records of their efforts over a period of time. It is extremely unlikely that either medical officers or educational psychologists will ever be in a position to gain the same knowledge, understanding and insights into a child, as teachers are able to achieve, collaboratively over a period of time. Teachers are therefore in a crucial position within the assessment procedure to contribute to the authority's awareness and determination of a child's special educational needs and the most appropriate form of provision to meet those needs. (Preparing information and writing advice are topics covered in Chapters 6 and 8 respectively.)

The Act itself says very little about the nature of the assessment process and the extent to which it should reflect emerging trends. No mention is made of how long the assessment should take (although this may change in the future) and how children's needs and desirable educational provision are to be identified. Circular 1/83 sheds some light on those issues but the actual phrasing within the Act does not embody the more recent and desirable forms of assessment.

After the advice had been submitted, and its recommendations considered, the LEA may decide that it is not necessary to determine the special educational provision that should be made for the child (i.e. not to produce a Statement of Special Educational Needs). The parents after being informed of this decision, may appeal in writing to the Secretary of State. Furthermore, it is the LEA who shall notify in writing the parent of this right. Following an appeal, the Secretary of State may, if he thinks fit, direct the LEA to reconsider their decision. It should be noted that the Secretary of State is not empowered to direct the authority to change its decision, only to suggest that it is reconsidered.

SECTION 7 STATEMENT OF CHILD'S SPECIAL EDUCATIONAL NEEDS

The circumstances described under Section 7 are closely related to events under Section 5, and the LEA's decision to initiate a formal assessment of a child's special educational needs. Where the assessment procedure has been completed and the LEA considers it appropriate to determine the special educational provision that should be made for a child, a Statement of his educational needs must be written and adhered to (in the terminology of the Act, the word used in this respect is maintained), *in such a manner as they consider appropriate*. The LEA is then duty-bound to ensure that the special educational provision specified in the Statement is made available (unless the child's parents have made suitable acceptable, alternative arrangements for his education).

Initially, any Statement prepared by the LEA is a provisional document. The draft copy is sent to the parent who may either accept it or disagree with any part of it and:

(a) **make representations (or further representations) to the authority about the content of the proposed statement;**
(b) **require the authority to arrange a meeting between him and an officer of the authority at which the proposed statement can be discussed.**

Subsection 4

The parent has 15 days from receiving the proposed Statement to make either representation or arrange a meeting with an officer of the authority. If this course of action is followed, the LEA after considering those representations may then:

(a) **make a statement in the form originally proposed;**
(b) **make a statement in a modified form; or**
(c) **determine not to make a statement.**

Subsection 8

Finally, once the decision to prepare a Statement has been taken, the LEA is then required to give the parents:

(a) **a copy of the statement;**
(b) **notice in writing of his right under Section 8(1) of this Act to appeal against the special educational provision specified in the statement; and**
(c) **notice in writing of the name of the person to whom he may apply for information and advice about the child's special educational needs.**

Subsection 9

Parents can therefore disagree with the proposed Statement and follow a number of channels to express their views. On some occasions this could mean parents request a meeting with members of the school staff responsible for compiling and submitting the advice. Ultimately, after taking into account the parents' representations, the authority can still proceed without carrying out any alterations and make the provisional Statement the completed one.

SECTION 8   APPEALS AGAINST STATEMENTS

Section 7 addressed itself to preparing a provisional Statement and the opportunities open to parents to discuss this before it becomes the completed Statement. Section 8 deals with the procedures to be followed when they want to appeal against the Statement issued by the LEA.

Parents may appeal to a local appeal committee, set up under the Education Act 1980. Parents can make representation to the committee who will consider the issues in relation to the LEA recommendations on how best to meet a child's special educational needs. When it comes to special educational provision, the appeal committee is not able to overrule the LEA's decision, if they disagree with the details of the Statement. What they are able to do is refer the case back to the authority with their observations and ask that the case be reviewed in the light of the committee's views. Alternatively, they can of course endorse the Statement and confirm the proposed special educational provision.

Should parents still feel dissatisfied with either of these decisions they may appeal, in writing to the Secretary of State. Three outcomes are then possible, after the Secretary of State has consulted with the LEA concerned. He may:

(a) **confirm the special educational provision specified in the statement;**
(b) **amend the statement so far as it specifies the special educational provision and make such other consequential amendments to the statement as he considers appropriate; or**
(c) **direct the LEA to cease to maintain the statement.**

Subsection 7

It is interesting to note that, under Section 5, the Secretary of State can only direct the LEA to reconsider its decision not to make appropriate provision to meet a child's special educational needs and prepare a Statement. Under Section 8, the Secretary of State has actual powers to amend the statement when he regards it as appropriate to do so.

SECTION 9   REQUESTS FOR ASSESSMENTS

Parents are able to approach the LEA and request that the LEA arranges for an assessment to be made of the child's educational needs. The authority is obliged to comply with this 'unless it is in their opinion unreasonable'. It is not clear from the Act what might constitute unreasonable grounds under these circumstances.

A summary of the main points of the Act appears in Table 3.1.

Table 3.1
Summary of the Sections of the 1981 Act

Section 1 Definitions
The terms defined are:
— special educational needs,
— learning difficulty,
— special educational provision.

Section 2 Provision
Duty of LEAs to see that children with special needs are educated in an ordinary school. Integration encouraged. All staff to be informed about a child having special educational needs. Duty of governors to ensure special education provision is made for an individual child.

Section 4 Duty of an LEA towards children for whom they are responsible
The LEA has to determine special educational provision for Statemented children.

Section 5 Assessment of Special Educational Needs
Deals with formal assessments and requests for advice from:
— teachers,
— educational psychologists,
— school medical officers.

Section 7 Statement of Child's Special Educational Needs
Covers the arrangements for LEAs intending to prepare a Statement on a child's special educational needs.

Section 8 Appeals Against Statements
Describes the procedures parents are to follow when appealing against a statement.

Section 9 Requests for Assessments
Gives parents the right to request an assessment from the LEA.

OTHER SECTIONS OF THE ACT

In the foregoing we have dealt with the main provisions of the Act as they apply to ordinary schools. The sections that we have not discussed focus on aspects of special education which are not the immediate concerns of teachers within the mainstream sector.

We summarise these as follows:

Section 3 discusses special educational provision which is made otherwise than in schools.

Section 6 deals with the assessment of special educational needs of children under the age of two. The LEA may where they feel a child less than two has special educational needs, or probably has, make an assessment of the child's needs with the consent of the parents and where appropriate provide a Statement.

Section 10 deals with the duty of an Area or District Health Authority to notify parents and the LEA of the probability that a child under the age of five has special educational needs.

Sections 11-14 deal with special schools and approved independent schools and *Sections 15-16* with school attendance orders.

Finally, *Sections 17-21* are termed Miscellaneous in the Act and describe:

— the duty of parents (Section 17),

— the powers of the Secretary of State with respect to requesting medical and other examinations (Section 18),

— how the regulations are to come into force or how they can be annulled. Furthermore the Regulations under this Act:

(c) may make different provision for different cases or circumstances;

(d) may contain such incidental, supplemental or transitional provisions as the Secretary of State thinks fit; and

(e) may make in relation to Wales provision different from that made in relation to England (Section 19).

— the terms "child" which 'includes any person who has not attained the age of 19 years and is registered as a pupil at a school'; "ordinary school" means a school which is not a special school; "principal Act" means the Education Act 1944 (Section 20).

— how the 1981 Education Act relates to previous Acts of Parliament (Section 21).

FURTHER READING

Cox, B. (1985). *The Law of Special Educational Needs: A Guide to the Education Act 1981,* Croom Helm, London.

An essentially legalistic rather than practical interpretation of the 1981 Act.

RESPONDING TO THE ACT: IMPLICATIONS FOR SCHOOLS

The preceding chapter described the legal provisions of the Act in so far as they applied to ordinary schools. In this chapter we look at the implications of the Act and how schools might plan to respond to its demands. Circular 1/83 (Assessments and Statements of Special Educational Needs) is the document that advises LEAs on:

> **the assessment of a broad range of special educational needs. It offers advice to assist LEAs in reviewing and revising their procedures in consultation with district health authorities and social services departments.**
>
> **Paragraph 1**

This circular can be taken to represent the view of the Department of Education and Science regarding:
— the principles governing good practice,
— the steps necessary to comply with the Act.

In total there are 75 paragraphs in the Circular covered by the following headings:
— General principles.
— Assessments in schools.
— Formal statutory procedures.
— Children under five.
— Language of instruction.
— Service children.
— Co-operation between education, social services and health authorities.

As in the previous chapter, we will again focus on those aspects of the Circular which are of particular relevance to ordinary schools.

The sections called General Principles and Assessments in Schools raise a number of overlapping and interrelated issues concerning good practice in schools. We have chosen to highlight five identifiable themes which we offer as a useful template with which to view the Circular. We will therefore look at each theme in turn and consider its implications.

The final part of the chapter focuses on the formal procedures which are to be followed, for the minority of pupils, whose educational needs are to be assessed under Section 5 of the Education Act.

In Chapters 1 and 3 we alluded to the ambiguities connected with the terminology of the Act and its related circulars. A number of these are evident in Circular 1/83 in particular and will be highlighted where there are relevant consequences for ordinary schools. The five prominent themes which we have identified are:
— identification and provision,
— involvement of other professionals,
— nature of assessment,
— record keeping and preparing reports,
— parental involvement.

However, before looking at each of the above themes, it is necessary to draw attention to the range of children referred to in Circular 1/83. One thing that is very clearly stated on the first page of the Circular is that the Act 'places a wider obligation on LEAs to secure that adequate provision is made for all children with special educational needs', (Paragraph 2), that is to say the much broader group of children, in Warnock's terms, the 20% of pupils who at some time during their school careers may have special educational needs. This is seen as one of the overriding principles of the 'new' view of special education and means attention is directed not just towards those children whose educational needs are being formally assessed under Section 5 of the Education Act, but also other pupils whose progress, for one reason or another, causes concern.

Circular 1/83 thus has implications for general classroom practice with ramifications which stretch beyond any immediate concerns for teaching children already identified as having special educational needs. A responsibility is placed on teachers to be aware that, potentially, any child could at some time have a special educational need. As a result teachers must be sensitive to the needs of all the children in the class and have systematic procedures developed to identify and monitor children's educational needs, whether they be regarded as 'special' or otherwise. The focus therefore is on laying the foundations for identifying, assessing and providing for the broader range of pupils within a school, as a principle of good practice. Out of this comes what might happen for the smaller group of children, approximately 2% according to Warnock, whose needs would be assessed under Section 5 of the Act. This particular issue leads us to a discussion of the first of the five prominent themes, identification and provision.

IDENTIFICATION AND PROVISION

The Circular states:

> **within individual schools, governors have a duty to secure that teachers are aware of the importance of identifying and providing for special educational needs. The teacher is directly responsible**

> for his pupils .... and to recognise the child who is experiencing difficulties in learning ....
>
> **Paragraph 11**

It is anticipated that:

> **Since every school is likely to have some pupils with special educational needs, LEAs should provide guidance to all maintained schools in their area on the arrangements for identifying, assessing and meeting special educational needs.**
>
> **Paragraph 8**

Individual schools therefore are encouraged to develop a system which enables teachers to become aware of the range of needs within the school population, especially those relating to children with special needs, and respond accordingly. Headteachers are clearly being encouraged to evolve a policy towards identifying special educational needs which operates throughout the school. In the past it has been possible for individual teachers to adopt their own methods of identification, without reference to colleagues or any overall framework existing within the school.

How children with special needs are identified will depend on a number of factors which will clearly then have a bearing on in-school provision. The school, in taking steps to evolve a policy, is faced with an immediate dilemma. What if a system is developed that has resource implications above and beyond what the school can presently meet with existing provision? Should the provision likely to be available influence decision making over how children with special needs are identified; a case of the tail wagging the dog! Of course the alternative of designing a process which creates a demand which cannot be met is equally frustrating.

How a problem such as this is eventually resolved will rest on a number of issues. Part of the decision making will involve the philosophy of the school with respect to children with special needs. To what extent is the principle of positive discrimination exercised in favour of these children? Is the relative importance which the head-teacher attaches to special needs represented through the use of resources and staffing? What kind of balance is to be achieved between policy decisions relating to special needs and other areas of the curriculum and school life? What level of competence, confidence and commitment exists within the staff as a whole? How will the inevitable additional planning and staff discussion time be viewed? Achieving an effective balance between the demands being created from outside through the Education Act and considering the preferences of staff, their professional development and areas of expertise, is in itself a delicate and dynamic process.

Nevertheless, the current legislation requires that some kind of response is made by the school which will subsequently influence how children with special needs are identified. A number of options present themselves ranging from the less to the more desirable. At one end of the continuum, the less acceptable systems can take the form of little more than casual observations. Sometimes these arise from hearing certain names crop up repeatedly in the staff room: 'Jimmy is a real trouble maker. He disrupts all the children in the class, never lets them get on with their work and inevitably never does any himself. He needs constant attention. It would be all right if I could devote all my time to him but I've got 29 others to think about. I just don't know what I'm going to do about him'.

Then at the end of the school year when the new class lists are passed around, the teacher finds to her horror that Jimmy is in her class next year. September comes around all too quickly, the new class assembles and the teacher expects the worst. Jimmy lives up to his reputation, disrupts everyone and by the end of the first term the teacher may be clamouring for something to be done.

Could the problem have been averted? Was Jimmy labelled from an early stage in his school career that gave rise to certain teacher expectations, which Jimmy duly conformed to? The dangers of labelling and the self-fulfilling prophecy are well documented (see Chapter 2, pp. 16–18) and are characteristic features of a particularly insidious form of identification. We have deliberately caricatured one route to identifying children with special needs, to highlight the dangers of decision making based on rumour, hearsay, expectation and pre-formulated opinions.

At the other end of the continuum is a process of identification where professional opinion is supported and illustrated by carefully collected records and information on the pupil. The records would form part of an on-going procedure, started when a child first attends the school. Included would be details of when any difficulties were first noted, the attempts made to overcome them and their respective outcomes. Discussion and consultations between staff having taught or currently teaching the pupil would be an integral part of the process. The views and opinions expressed however, would be backed up by systematic and detailed classroom observation.

The topic of identification is closely related to current thinking about assessment and is therefore an area which shall be looked at again and developed later in this chapter and in Chapters 5 and 6.

Also, inextricably linked to the identification of children with special needs, is the determination of appropriate provision to meet those needs. This will as we have already mentioned be affected by the number of children identified, existing staffing levels, teacher expertise in the area and possibly availability of support services. These factors together with general school policy give rise to several options for organising provision, some of which will now be considered briefly.

Class-based Provision With No Additional Personnel

The class teacher undertakes all special needs teaching within her own classroom. To be successful this will inevitably involve commitment to some degree of positive discrimination in favour of the identified children. This will be required in two ways, one of which will in all probability make a greater demand on time, than the other.

In the classroom, some time will need to be created by the teacher to carry out individual or group teaching, depending on the number of children identified. Other children will have to be gainfully occupied during those teaching periods, preferably on activities, which as far as can be anticipated in advance, can be completed without too much teacher assistance. Finding time to undertake uninterrupted work with a selected group of pupils for a period of time is a perennial issue for the class teacher. Teachers often have to find time to work with individual children. For example, listening to them read, discussing a book they have enjoyed, clarifying aspects of work being undertaken, etc. This issue is brought into sharper focus when the children have 'special needs'.

Frequently, time also has to be found outside normal teaching hours. Programmes of work may need to be evaluated and adapted, materials may need preparing, and consultation may be necessary with teaching colleagues and LEA support services. Moreover the possibility of school-focused INSET or staff development may be considered to increase awareness and effectiveness. There is no easy answer to the question 'how much additional time is likely to be involved?' All that can be said reliably is that the demands created by the new legislation will require that some time is set aside both inside and outside the classroom, for planning and implementing special programmes of work.

Class-based Provision With Additional Personnel Available

Additional personnel to work in conjunction with the class teacher may become available in a number of ways. Similarly, there are numerous options on how to deploy the extra staffing. A policy decision may dictate that one teacher will be given the responsibility for part, or possibly the whole school day, to work in different classrooms, in collaboration with the class teacher to teach those pupils experiencing difficulties. Alternatively, the additional member of staff could work with the whole class for a certain period of time, thus freeing the class teacher to concentrate on the pupil(s) with special needs. The actual practicalities of the arrangement will inevitably depend on individual teachers' experience and background.

The flexible use of staff, to be successful, involves a significant commitment on the part of *all* the teachers in a school, as it has inevitable implications for them even if they themselves are not directly receiving any additional assistance for special needs children. For one teacher to be without a class for part of the school day means that colleagues may have additional children in their classrooms. In order that feelings of resentment are not generated by thoughts along the lines of 'Why has X got extra help and not me?', the rationale for making this type of provision has to be explicity articulated and discussed among staff.

Increasingly, ancillary staff and parents have been engaged to lend assistance in classrooms in a non-teaching capacity. They do not take responsibility for organising what is taught or deciding how to teach, but under the general direction of the class teacher may, for example, supervise a group activity, listen to children read or help with materials. This can free the class teacher for brief periods to work with a smaller number of children without the immediate pressure of being forever 'on call'.

This form of provision has a number of appealing features. It takes place in the child's usual environment, the classroom, and can be implemented with few disruptions to the daily classroom routines of the children. It has the potential to foster closer working relationships between teachers when skills and expertise are shared. Any disadvantages could be overcome within the context of a commitment and continuing, positive dialogue amongst staff.

Withdrawing Children from the Classroom

With this form of provision, children are taken out of the classroom environment for what are usually brief periods during the school day. They may be taught either individually or in a small group, depending on their needs and on the overall demand. The problems connected with this type of provision with respect to their educational and social consequences have been well documented (e.g. Fish, 1985).

Children who are withdrawn may feel uncomfortable about having to leave the classroom. They could feel 'in the spotlight' and that undue attention is being focused upon them and their difficulties. The need for close co-operation between the class and 'withdrawal' teacher is essential. There is a real risk here that the class teacher may 'breathe a sigh of relief' in the knowledge that the child is receiving extra help. Unless there is an active collaboration between the class teacher and the withdrawal teacher concerning the particular programme of work, the help may be *in place of* rather than *supplementary* to normal classroom teaching.

When this works well, preparation is genuinely shared as is the responsibility for meeting the child's needs. The class teacher and specialist withdrawal teacher can compare their professional opinions of the pupil's performance in different settings, and thereby arrive at a more detailed appreciation of the most suitable provision for a child.

Special Classes and Units

In this form of provision, whether it be for those with learning or behaviour problems, the children may spend some or all of their school day in a separate class or group with others experiencing difficulties. A special unit is something of a half-way house between an ordinary and special school. Teaching is usually the responsibility of a single member of the staff with a specialist background in the area. Also the content of the curriculum is frequently different from that available in the rest of the school.

This form of provision raises issues of integration, relationships between unit teachers and mainstream colleagues and the curriculum to be followed and has been the centre of much recent debate within LEAs. Topping (1983) has reviewed the role of such classes in some detail.

The question of identifying special educational needs and making appropriate provision clearly has major implications for *all* the teachers in a school. It is essential that an overall school policy is developed which addresses itself to the following three questions:
— what information is available to a school to describe the needs of the population it serves?
— what internal processes can a school use to identify children who might have special educational needs?
— what organisational and resource options are most appropriate to meet children's special educational needs?

EARLY INTERVENTION AND THE PROGRESSIVE INVOLVEMENT OF OTHER PROFESSIONALS

The Warnock Report (DES, 1978) proposed a five stage procedure for intervening and involving the expertise of support services. DES Circular 1/83 endorses the view that LEA assessment procedures 'should allow for the progressive extension of professional involvement from the class teacher to the headteacher, a specialist teacher, the educational psychologist, the school doctor and nurse and other professionals in the education, health and social services'. Before looking at the Warnock five stages, we will briefly describe the professionals with whom a teacher might have contact within the terms of reference of Circular 1/83 and the 1981 Education Act.

Educational Psychologists

Educational psychologists are employed by the LEA usually within School Psychological Services. They have a degree in psychology, are qualified teachers with a minimum of two years relevant teaching experience and have undertaken post-graduate training in educational psychology. They are involved in a wide range of activities in relation to children with special needs. They are available to advise teachers and parents informally about children who may be experiencing learning or behavioural difficulties, or may become more actively and closely involved with particular children when systematically assessing their educational needs. In many LEAs, they also provide in-service training courses for teachers (for example on school-based assessment techniques, teaching and behavioural management approaches). Their role within LEAs is continually developing and services may vary in the way they are organised. However, they all have an important role under the Act and are required to submit advice when an assessment is initiated under Section 5.

School Medical Officers

School medical offers are fully qualified doctors, employed by the District Health Authority to advise the LEA on the medical side of children's development. They also act as the link between the education department and the wider provision available within the health service, for example: various medical specialists, paediatricians, physiotherapists, speech therapists, etc. They do not actually treat children themselves, but when the need arises are in a position to ensure that access is available to the appropriate specialist. They also prepare and submit advice to LEAs under Section 5 on behalf of the Health Authority. Some medical officers may have a special role, for example, within a multidisciplinary team for assessing pre-school children with possible handicaps.

Learning Support Teachers

Most LEAs provide teams of teachers to support classroom teachers in their work with children with special needs. These are frequently known as the Remedial Service or Learning Support Service. Help may be provided in a variety of ways: withdrawing children for extra teaching on a one-to-one or small group basis, working alongside the class teacher, guiding schools in the choice of material resources available. Such services may also operate special teaching units for children with difficulties and take part in in-service training of teachers in mainstream schools.

Many authorities also provide specialist advisory teachers for children with sensory handicap (vision, hearing) and for pre-school and nursery-aged children who may be showing signs of developmental delay.

Educational Inspectors and Advisers

Inspectors and advisers are employed by the LEA to provide general and specialist advice for schools on such issues as curriculum development, dissemination of good practice, staffing, the implications of regional and national initiatives, government legislation, etc. They also assist the authority in determining its policy on such issues. They are expected to have a role in monitoring the quality of education provided by the LEA.

Many LEAs will have a specialist inspector or adviser who is responsible for providing advice regarding the provision for pupils with special needs, both in ordinary and special schools or units.

Assistant Education Officers for Special Education

Each LEA has a number of Assistant Education Officers (AEOs), one of whom will usually have particular responsibility for special education. The AEO co-ordinates the administrative side of the Act on behalf of the Director of Education to whom he is directly responsible. The AEO ensures that notification is given that a Section 5 assessment is to be undertaken and that the necessary documents are sent to the appropriate people. The AEO also has a much wider role to see that, administratively, special education (special schools and support services) is effectively organised within the LEA according to its policy.

Statements Officer

Every LEA will have a Statements Officer (SO), although the precise status of this officer may vary from authority to authority. In some LEAs, the role may be performed by educational psychologists, in others by the adviser for special education and in some, by a specially appointed person with no other responsibilities or duties within the LEA. The SO could therefore be a person with considerable practical experience in special education but could also be someone with little or no relevant teaching or professional background in special needs.

After the LEA has decided that it should make provision to meet a child's special educational needs, the SO has the task of drafting the provisional Statement on the basis of the advice received. Subsequently this will either be confirmed as the completed Statement or amendments will be made.

Psychiatrist

A psychiatrist is a fully qualified doctor who has received further training in the area of mental health. The majority of psychiatrists work predominantly with adults but some specialise in working with children and their families. They are usually hospital-based but may also have a base at a LEA Child Guidance Centre. They focus on a range of social and emotional problems which children and adolescents may present, for example: anorexia, depression, which they might respond to in a variety of ways (e.g. psychotherapy, family therapy).

Paediatrician

A paediatrician is also a fully qualified doctor who has specialised in childhood problems of a physical rather than mental nature, for example: cerebral palsy, Down's syndrome, muscular dystrophy. They are most likely to have contact with teachers in the primary sector and in particular, teachers in special schools or units for children with physical or developmental problems.

Speech Therapists

Speech therapists will have a degree or diploma in speech therapy. Their main role is to provide treatment for children experiencing serious difficulties in speech articulation and language development. In the past, speech therapists have tended to work with individual children at a Health Authority clinic. Over recent years, many speech therapists have worked more closely with the child's teacher, acting in an advisory capacity and providing support material for use in the classroom where appropriate.

Social Workers

The majority of social workers are employed by Social Services Departments, though some may be employed by LEAs. They come from a variety of backgrounds. Some will have degrees in sociology or psychology, but others may have graduated in an unrelated subject. A degree is not mandatory and some social workers will have had considerable practical experience in various aspects of social services provision in an untrained capacity. The main social work qualifiction is the Certificate for Qualification in Social Work (CQSW). Social workers work with individuals and families and have a range of statutory functions which are not related to the education system, but there may well be occasions when they are involved in contributing to the statutory assessment procedure. This will, in general, be in a limited number of instances when an understanding of the child's home circumstances might contribute to a more comprehensive appreciation of his educational needs. Unlike educational psychologists, school medical officers and teachers, social workers do not automatically submit advice to LEAs as part of a Section 5 assessment, but may do so when requested.

The Warnock Report's Five Stages of Assessment

The Warnock Report proposed a five stage model for the progressive involvement of teaching and advisory personnel. These are:
(1) The class teacher and headteacher collect information about the child, discuss the nature of the difficuties with the parents and consider how the school might, with its current provision, meet the child's needs.
(2) A special education teacher from either the school or from a visiting service contributes to (1) above, in the form of an assessment and

looks at how the child's needs might be met with existing resources but possibly including help from the special education teacher.

(3) A specialist from outside the school, perhaps an educational psychologist, school doctor, social worker, etc. carries out an assessment which is additional to (1) and (2). At this stage a decision is taken about whether the existing provision can meet the child's needs, whether additional professional help is required from outside the school or whether referral for assessment by a multi-professional team would be appropriate.

(4) Any multi-professional assessment would include medical, psychological and educational components. Views of other professionals could also be sought where relevant.

(5) Centres to be established where multi-professional assessments can take place on children with complex problems which require a more specialised and detailed assessment than is likely to be possible under (4). Since the 1981 Act, Warnock's stages (4) and (5) correspond to the statutory assessment procedure (see Chapter 7).

The five stages emphasise the importance of teachers being able to identify children's needs and in the first instance, of schools trying to meet those needs with existing resources. While this is an appropriate first step, Warnock's view of successive stages could lead to other professionals not being involved until it was too late, that is when a situation had become critical. Many professionals would prefer to be involved as early as possible, perhaps just for informal consultations, so that they too could determine the most appropriate time to become involved. Early professional contact would not necessarily pre-empt stages (1), (2) and (3) but should be seen instead as complementary to existing attempts to establish a pupil's needs. The five stages can best be viewed as a range of options as to who might appropriately contribute to an assessment, rather than as a strict order for their involvement.

We would also see this as the most acceptable way of extending professional involvement under the Education Act. Nothing will be lost and there is a great deal to be gained by contacting the appropriate professional as early as possible before any problem becomes too serious. Circular 1/83 makes it clear that LEAs ought to notify schools of the specialist services available for referrals, together with details of channels of communication.

One of the prerequisites of effective inter-disciplinary work is for detailed records to be kept of children's progress, collected over as long a period as possible. The contribution which a professional from an external agency can make will invariably only be as good as the information which he or she has to work on. An analogous situation exists when visiting a doctor or dentist or even taking your car to the garage to be repaired. The more details that can be given to describe the ailment, the more appropriate the intervention is likely to be.

Working with Colleagues

One final word on the support services available to teachers. Discussions on this topic invariably tend to focus on agencies which are external to the school and yet a very well informed, immediate support group is available in the form of teaching colleagues.

Teaching can be an isolated profession with individual teachers tending to keep many of the issues that concern them to themselves. It is not uncommon, in some schools, for teachers rarely to share and discuss their professional concerns in an open way with colleagues. Teaching in such a context is frequently lonely and disheartening.

We would see that, potentially, the most valuable source of support available to teachers is their teaching colleagues. Teachers working co-operatively, forming interest groups, 'brainstorming' problems, sharing experiences, not only create positive models for children to observe, but help foster a school ethos based on collaborative working and mutual support and acceptance.

ASSESSMENT

Many references are made in Circular 1/83 to the process of 'assessment'. However, careful analysis of the relevant sections reveals a number of ambiguities about what might actually be involved in assessing a child's educational needs. In this section we will describe the features of the assessment process conveyed in the circular and then highlight the areas which need developing and clarifying.

According to Circular 1/83
(a) The main 'focus (of assessment) should be on the child himself rather than on his disability' (Paragraph 3). It should identify not only his strengths and weaknesses but also his personal resources and attributes together with the 'nature of his interaction with his environment' (Paragraph 3).
(b) Assessment is not an end in itself, 'but a means of arriving at a better understanding of a child's learning difficulties for the practical purpose of providing a guide to his education and a basis against which to monitor his progress' (Paragraph 4).
(c) 'Assessment is a continuous process' (Paragraph 5). This is reiterated in Paragraph 10, 'all parties should remember that assessment is not a single event but a continuous process'.
(d) 'Assessment should be seen as a partnership between teachers, other professionals, and parents, in a joint endeavour to discover and understand the nature of the difficulties and needs of individual children (Paragraph 6). Paragraph 10 further emphasises, 'other professionals should work together with the teacher'.
(e) 'Assessment should always be closely related to education' (Paragraph 10).

Assessment is thus seen as a continuous process, which should focus on the child, his strengths and weaknesses, his personal attributes and resources and take into account his interaction with his environment. The process is a partnership between teacher, professionals and parents who work together to gain a better understanding of the child's difficulties. Finally, assessment is directly related to a child's education and should provide a guide to future education and provision.

In order to achieve these aims, the Circular recognises the importance of the teacher's role. The teacher is in many ways the central figure in the assessment, being the person with whom other professionals are required to work. This theme is developed in Paragraph 11 which appreciates the unique perspective of the teacher: 'he is in a key position to observe their (the children's) response in the classroom, to recognise the child who is experiencing learning difficulties, and to try out different approaches to help meet the child's needs'.

The Circular appears to make the assumption that children whose needs are being assessed definitely have a learning difficulty (see a, b and d, above). To make such a judgement appears a little premature. Surely the purpose of the assessment is to try and establish whether the difficulties encountered by a child do in fact represent a 'real' rather than 'hypothesised' difficulty in learning, that is: 'significantly greater than the majority of children of his age' (Education Act 1981, Section 1, Subsection 2. To state the child has a 'learning difficulty' as is done in the Circular, both pre-empts and undermines the purpose of assessment.

A second area which requires some discussion is the one concerning the relationship between educational need and provision. The distinction between the two is crucial to an understanding of the Act. The Circular tackles the issue in Paragraph 4:

> Whilst assessment should take account of provision, it is important that a clear distinction should be made in future between:
> (a) the analysis of the child's learning difficulties;
> (b) the specification of his special needs for different kinds of approaches, facilities, or resources;
> (c) the determination of the special educational provision to meet these needs.

What is not clear from the Circular is how the progression occurs from (a) to (b). Let us consider the problem for a moment. It is implied that an analysis of the child's learning difficulties will lead to a specification of his special needs. It seems to us unlikely that this could be achieved without the inclusion of an additional step.

What could be concluded following an analysis of a child's learning difficulties? It might be found, for instance, that the difficulties arose from poor attendance and rarely being at school, or the discovery that the child suffered a severe hearing loss which had previously been undetected. Does knowing that a hearing impairment was a major contributory factor to the child's difficulties lead to a clear specification of his educational needs? To say that he needs either a hearing aid or placement in a special school for the deaf or partially hearing, is in fact to describe *a form of provision*. We would still want to know what the child needs to be taught, i.e. what does the child lack that it is felt essential that he learns. He may need to be taught various mathematical, reading or language concepts, areas of the curriculum where it is likely the difficulties were first noticed. Finding the answer to these questions comes from a different type of analysis, that of finding out what the child can and cannot do in relation to different aspects of the curriculum and social demands.

An analysis of the child's difficulties may therefore help in identifying appropriate forms of provision. However, it does not indicate what social academic skills the child has learned or what should be taught next. It is the skills the child lacks that reflect his educational needs, not only the explanation for his difficulties.

The point can be clarified by looking at an example from everyday life. Let us suppose we are feeling hungry. An analysis of why we are hungry could lead us to think it is because it is several hours since our last meal or because we have just walked past our favourite restaurant and can readily conjure up images of the food served there. Following the analysis we might conclude that we want something to eat. This will be the provision to meet the need, our feelings of hunger. However, we have not answered the question of what we want to eat or may need to eat. The answer to this will depend on the extent of our hunger, when our next meal is due and what may be good for our digestive system. We can only decide what to eat after considering a series of questions which are independent of our analysis of why we are hungry.

The confusion arises because the Circular does not provide any clear indication of what is meant by 'the analysis of the child's learning difficulties'. However, the suggested checklist for advice on special needs provided in Annex 1 of the Circular (shown in Appendix 1) suggests a descriptive analysis. Whilst it invites the school to provide details of the child's functioning, aims of provision, and facilities and resources, nowhere does it invite a specification of need!

We would suggest that there are *two possible types of analysis*. The one implied in the Circular, which we would call a *descriptive analysis*, leads to a description of what is wrong with the child and to appropriate provision being identified. A second form, that we refer to as assessment-through-teaching in Chapter 5, looks at *what the child needs to be taught* as well as identifying suitable provision, i.e. how best to teach him and what learning experiences to provide.

An extra step has to be inserted between (a) and (b) in Circular 1/83 which seeks to find out what skills the child has already learned and what needs to be learned next. Only then will we be in a position to comment confidently on the most appropriate provision to meet needs. A detailed analysis of a learning difficulty can help to identify forms of appropriate provision, but this will not necessarily contribute to an understanding of the child's educational needs.

The issue is complicated by everyday language and the way the term 'need' is frequently used, especially in educational circles. We might talk about a child needing a structured curriculum, or needing a placement in a special school or needing a particular approach to the management of his behaviour. Each of these is a form of provision and because they are what a child needs, there is the temptation to blur the distinction between need and provision. They beg the question, 'Why does the child require a structured curriculum or placement in a special school or particular approach to management?' An answer to this question must be based on *an appraisal of what the child has learned, what he should be taught next and careful observation of how the child responds to different teaching arrangements and learning experiences.*

This notion of assessment would apply equally whatever theoretical model of learning or teaching is adopted, since in the final analysis we have to reach a decision about what is to be taught next and how it is to be taught. Thus, apart from this lack of clarity the general principles of effective assessment represented elsewhere in the Circular also apply to any theoretical view of the nature of children's learning. These can be summarised as:
— being continuous,
— taking into account a child's personal attributes and resources,
— considering the way he interacts with his environment,
— being a partnership between teacher, professionals and parents,
— being related to education,
— trying out different approaches to help meet the child's needs.

RECORD KEEPING

> **Teachers should be encouraged to keep full records of the pupils' progress and to include information about professional consultations and assessments.**
>
> **Paragraph 11**

What might this mean in practice and how does it relate to possible interpretations regarding the functions of record keeping?

There are many ways of keeping records on children's progress, some of which would probably be regarded as desirable by a majority of teachers and others which would be viewed less favourably. When thinking of the type of record keeping envisaged in the Circular, it is useful to bear in mind the purpose to which they will be put. The records kept are likely to form the basis of the school's advice offered to an LEA under Section 5 of the Act. The data collected is likely therefore to be examined closely by advisors, AEOs and the Statements Officer. If a provisional Statement is prepared, the school's advice would be made available to parents, as it would be to an Appeals Committee, the Secretary of State or perhaps even a Court of Law, should the parents invoke their right to appeal at any of the specified stages in the procedure. It is clearly imperative that schools should therefore consider that the records they keep give a valid and representative account of the work they have undertaken with the child experiencing difficulties.

The nature of the assessment process as conveyed in the Circular, implies that records should be kept over a period of time, be closely related to the child's educational programme and indicate what happened as different approaches were tried to help meet the child's needs. They should therefore document what the child has learned and typical responses to the teaching approaches adopted. Teaching in this context may be seen as experimental as the teacher tries one method, records the child's progress and evaluates the effectiveness of the intervention. Decisions regarding future teaching can then be based on this information, any changes made to the teaching programme or patterns of classroom organisation being noted. Over a period of time a picture may emerge of which teaching strategies are most effective with individual children. The child's actual progress, achieved with the provision available, can then be compared with what might be considered optimal and other available forms of provision.

This view of record keeping also has curriculum implications. It will be necessary to plan in advance and know what is going to be taught. This means articulating what the child is to learn and trying to tailor the curriculum to meet the child's needs. Part of the 'experimental' perception of teaching involves a willingness to look carefully at the curriculum to see whether it contributes in any way to the difficulties being experienced.

Record keeping is not a static process divorced from the process of teaching. What is envisaged is a long way from hastily compiled records, written at the end of term and based essentially on *recollections* of the events of the past year. Record keeping is an essential and integral part of teaching generally and the assessment period in particular. What is taught, how it is taught and what children learn as a result, have to be monitored and evaluated as often as possible. This provides the key to identifying needs and appropriate provision.

One further point needs stressing. This Circular is advancing principles of good practice which are not related to any specific model of children's learning or teaching process. What has been discussed in relation to record keeping is applicable to any theoretical orientation applied in the classroom. We would recognise that teachers favour different styles of teaching and also vary in how they interpret the educational needs of individual pupils. Nevertheless, it is important that the assessment and the resulting records reflect the spirit of Circular 1/83.

PARENTAL INVOLVEMENT

The nature of parents' involvement is described in the following terms by Circular 1/83

> **Assessment should be seen as a partnership between teachers, other professionals and parents ... Close relations should be established and maintained with parents and can only be helped by frankness and openness on all sides.**
>
> **Paragraph 6**

Similarly when referring to the involvement of other professionals, the Circular states:

> **The child's parents should be involved and kept fully informed at every stage.**
>
> **Paragraph 9**

Schools are therefore exhorted to involve parents throughout the assessment procedure within an honest and open relationship. It is to be hoped that how a school works with a parent within the framework of the Act, is no different from the way this responsibility is usually undertaken. It is difficult to imagine how the required levels of frankness and openness could be achieved without it. This is yet another example of the Circular emphasising principles and elements of good practice which apply to all aspects of teaching, and not just those connected with special education.

However, in saying this, the nature of a school's contact with parents within the framework of the Act is frequently very different from that experienced at other times. Being made aware that their child is having difficulties is likely to be painful for parents to accept. For them the period of assessment is an uncertain one and likely to provoke feelings of anxiety. It is not uncommon for teachers to experience parents becoming defensive at times such as these. Parents may interpret their child's problems as directly related to them in some way, possibly feeling it is 'their fault', or become unduly critical of the school.

A school therefore needs to be sensitive to how parents might view events and think how they can generate the most supportive atmosphere in their contact with them. How can an effective partnership be developed which accommodates the principles outlined in the Circular? This important area is discussed in some detail in Chapter 9.

SUMMARY

A number of implications for good practice can be drawn from the points arising from the discussion of these five themes. They highlight the need to collect data on all aspects of teaching children thought to have special educational needs. The data form the basis of future advice, are essential for successful collaborative working with colleagues and will be required when negotiating with other professionals.

Teachers must formulate effective procedures for identifying children who might have special educational needs and co-ordinate the involvement of other professions. Their responsibility for working closely with parents during the assessment is also fully recognised. Amongst all the professionals involved, teachers play a key role in assessment. They alone have prolonged contact with the child who presents problems and are therefore in a position to gain a crucial understanding of the child and his educational needs.

Assessment is no longer something done by 'experts' outside the classroom. It now takes on an entirely different form and teachers are central to the whole process. It is *they* rather than psychologists, advisers or school medical officers who have the responsibility for implementing the major part of the assessment and ensuring that the spirit of the Act is translated into effective classroom practice.

FURTHER READING

Brennan, W. (1987). *Changing Special Education Now*, Open University Press, Milton Keynes.

> Looks at the ways in which special educational needs can be met in both ordinary and special schools.

Gulliford, R. (1985). *Teaching Children with Learning Difficulties*, N.F.E.R. – Nelson, Windsor.

> An introduction to the field of learning difficulties and a practical summary of the implications of recent developments and legislation.

Pearson, L. and Lindsay, G. (1986). *Special Needs in the Primary School: Identification and Intervention*, N.F.E.R. – Nelson, Windsor.

> A guide to some strategies and specific procedures available to teachers for implementing the 1981 Act.

Wolfendale, S. (1987). *Primary Schools and Special Needs: Policy Planning and Provision*, Cassell, London.

The stated concern of this book is to explore the ways in which ordinary primary schools can meet the special needs of their pupils.

Chapter Five

TEACHING AND ASSESSMENT

Within the field of education and special education in particular, the term 'assessment' conjures up a wide range of perceptions and attitudes about children, the types of assessment procedures adopted to clarify and explain their difficulties and the involvement of other professionals. At one time when dealing with children experiencing problems the main responsiblity placed on teachers was to liaise with parents, perhaps notify the LEA and call upon the expertise of a member of the support services, which might often be a remedial specialist department or educational psychologist. The 'expert' would then be expected to 'assess' the child and offer an explanation for the difficulties encounted and provide proposals for appropriate remediation.

A predominant feature of this approach to assessment was the attempt to classify and categorise children according to their handicap. It aimed to find out what was 'wrong' with them and inevitably led to pupils being labelled. This view of assessment also carried with it a number of expectations. The assessment was seen to take place outside the classroom by members of other professions who were thought to have greater expertise than teachers in diagnosing the nature of children's difficulties and identifying their educational needs. It was less likely to be experienced as a collaborative venture between teachers, other professionals and parents. Parental permission would be sought from parents but their involvement could often be peripheral. They were expected to receive and accept the professional judgements of the experts rather than make a contribution to the whole process.

The assessment usually took place on a single occasion and was often unrelated to the classroom activities most familiar to the child. These circumstances created a number of pressures for the pupil. The pupil was expected to perform at an optimal level with a previously unknown person, in an unfamiliar environment on a range of strange activities. At the end of the assessment and after a due period of deliberation on the part of the tester, a written report might be submitted to the school, outlining the main conclusions and possible recommendations for future action.

Before looking at the issues surrounding the development of this form of assessment, it is useful to consider the questions that usually required answers when concerns were expressed about a child's progress. Some could be answered by the class teacher. However, it was thought others were best answered by personnel from the visiting support services.

The questions can also be looked at in terms of whether answers were formulated from information derived from the nature of the curriculum and teaching approaches used or those not directly related to the teaching process at all. Solutions to this latter group of questions were frequently based on the use of standardised tests (usually attainment, intelligence or diagnostic tests) which were administered by the educational psychologist. They are listed in Table 5.1.

Table 5.1
Questions to be Answered by Attainment, Diagnostic and Intelligence Tests

Is he behind?
How far behind?
Does he have a learning difficulty?
Does he have a specific learning difficulty?
Is he capable of learning more quickly?
Will he catch up with his peers?
Is he reaching his potential? Or is he underachieving?

QUESTIONS TO BE ANSWERED BY ATTAINMENT, DIAGNOSTIC AND INTELLIGENCE TESTS

Is He Behind?

This question raises the contentious issue of comparing one child's level of performance with that of his immediate peer group. What is being referred to are the pupil's current attainment levels and their relationship to those of other children in the class or children of similar age elsewhere in the school. Have the child's levels of skill acquisition in basic academic skills fallen behind those of peers? Have other children progressed further along the curriculum in the important areas of reading, writing, language and numeracy?

How Far Behind?

Related to the first question are concerns about how far a child is behind his peers in particular areas of school attainment. The extent to which a gap in attainment levels exists between one child, or even a small group of children and the rest of the class, has immediate curriculum and management implications. Different schemes of work and organisational arrangements for teaching might be necessary in order to compensate for, or remedy the child's disadvantage.

Does He Have a Learning Difficulty?

An assumption frequently made when a child is seen to be behind his peers in learning early literacy and numeracy skills, is that the gap is attributable to a learning difficulty. There are many reasons why such a situation might arise, not all of which are created through a pupil having a difficulty in learning. There may have been prolonged absences or changes of school which interrupted the child's education. Equally, merely attending school and sitting through lessons does not automatically mean a pupil is actively *engaged* in learning. Work might be too hard, the pupil's attention may wander, instructions could be too complex or the child might not be interested in the presented activities and as a result lack motivation.

The fact that a child has not *acquired* the same skills as peers should not therefore be taken as automatic proof that the child has a difficulty in *learning*. A more valid type of investigation which would help to establish whether this indeed was the case, would involve closely monitoring his performance in relation to what was being taught, over a period. Assessment can be likened to photographs: the 'snapshot' presents a single picture caught in time; the 'video' presents a picture in context. In our view, the notion of assessment as a 'video recording' is to be preferred.

Does He Have a Specific Learning Difficulty?

On occasions, when a closer analysis of the nature of the problems encountered by a pupil suggests they have arisen through a difficulty in learning, the extent of the difficulty will need to be ascertained. Is the problem confined to one curriculum area or is it more general, affecting the child's performance in several areas?

Is He Capable of Learning More Quickly?

In Chapter 2 we took a brief look at the history of special education and discussed the ways children we now describe as having special needs have been referred to previously. One of the terms used was 'ineducable'. The development of special schools was based in part on this assumption that some children are not able to learn or not able to learn very much. It was argued that time should not be wasted within the ordinary school teaching children who were not capable of learning. It would be better to concentrate efforts and resources on those pupils who could learn and could therefore benefit from the teaching received.

Deciding whether the child could learn was a question answered in conjunction with the previous one about fulfilling potential. Again the question is valid but, we would suggest needs to be looked at in a slightly different way. It is relevant to know how *quickly* a child learns and the conditions under which *optimal* learning takes place, as this enables appropriate provision to be made to meet the pupil's needs. It is the means by which an answer is sought in the light of the new legislation that is important.

Will the Child Catch Up with his Peers?

The answer to this question revolves round two important issues. The first centres on the child's 'potential' for learning, which is discussed in the next section. The second relates to the extent to which a child can bridge the gap in attainment levels that exists between him and his peers.

For a child to catch up with his peers, his rate of learning has to be *accelerated*. This is to say, he would actually have to learn at a rate which is quicker that that of this peers. Other children will not be standing still in their acquisition of new skills but continuing to learn as they did previously. The pupil who has fallen behind must therefore learn more rapidly in order that he has a chance to catch up with his peers. Whether or not this happens will depend, in part, on the effectiveness of the child's learning environment and the way it is organised to meet his specific educational needs.

Is He Reaching His Potential? Or Is He Underachieving?

A question frequently asked is whether children are 'fulfilling their potential'. This is predicated on the assumption that children have a maximum level of performance, both in terms of what they are able to learn and the rate at which new learning can occur. When this hypothesised level of performance in ascertained, it is argued, it is possible to say whether a child's difficulty in learning is simply the result of her having fulfilled her potential, i.e. the pupil is learning as quickly as she can and it is unlikely that any further or modified teaching, regardless of its quality, can change matters.

In the past it has been the educational psychologist who has been asked to 'measure potential', usually by the administration of an intelligence test. The results of a child's performance are expressed as an Intelligence Quotient (IQ). The assumption here would be that the higher a pupil's score, the greater the likelihood of future teaching being effective, since higher levels of IQ are associated with greater learning potential and future scholastic achievement.

The use of IQ tests in this way has been increasingly questioned in recent years (see Chapter 2) and they are now much less likely to form part of an educational psychologist's assessment of a child's special educational needs. However, the question is still relevant. What is required is a different approach to formulating an answer to it, which is not based on the administration of IQ tests.

A child might therefore be seen to be *behind* in several ways. The child's performance in literacy and numeracy may not be up to the same standard as other children in the class. In this sense he is behind his immediate peer group.

At the same time, attainment tests present fixed levels of achievement that are age-related and imply minimum levels of performance to be reached at different ages. A child might therefore also be seen to be behind these hypothesised levels of achievement.

People might choose to base expectations about future performance on measured levels of intelligence. Knowing what this might be for a child could lead to predictions about future attainments. Where a child is not learning in the way that has been expected, the conclusion reached might be that the child is not fulfilling his potential; that although behind the hypothesised level of achievement, improvements could reasonably be anticipated on the basis of his intelligence. However, a child whose attainments were behind those of peers might be viewed as *retarded* if his measured intelligence level was low and give rise to the expectation that his attainments in numeracy and literacy would also be low.

Related to questions about whether children are fulfilling their potential is the issue of underachievement. Again the argument runs along similar lines. If children are seen to have a high capacity for learning (i.e. they have an above average IQ) and yet are performing poorly (below average) in one or more basic skill area, it would be argued that the child is underachieving. The above average IQ would create the expectation that the child should be able to read, write, etc. at an above average level also. The notion of underachievement is therefore closely connected to the administration of IQ tests, identifying potential for learning and then seeing whether academic performance is commensurate with these expectations.

Two very different *types* of tests have been used to address the questions and issues we have raised. These are norm-referenced (normative) and criterion-referenced tests.

NORMATIVE TESTS

Normative tests are designed to compare one child's level of performance with those of other children. Initially, when a normative test is being prepared, the test designer selects items which it is thought represent the skills or attributes under investigation.

What is crucial to an understanding of normative tests is the criteria by which items are selected for inclusion in the final version following initial trials. Essentially, items are judged according to whether they contribute positively to achieving a normal distribution of scores. This could therefore mean that certain items might be rejected because they do not do this, even though they may be important skills for children to learn. In this sense a normative test is not curriculum-based. Items are selected on the basis of their ability to discriminate between pupils and provide results fitting the normal distribution (see Figure 5.1). It is their efficiency in this role that is of importance.

A pilot test is prepared which is then given to a random sample of individuals, with whom future comparisons are made. The idea is to include as many people as possible in the random sample who reflect the characteristics of the groups the test will be used with. The aim of this process it to put together a range of test items which when given to a large number of children yield results conforming to a 'normal

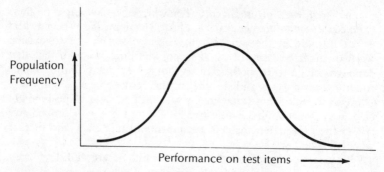

Figure 5.1   The normal distribution.

distribution' (see Figure 5.1).

The notion of a normal distribution rests on the assumption that the vast majority of children will achieve results which cluster round a middle point, with fewer achieving at the extremes (very high or very low performances). In a typical standardised test, the scores are *adjusted* so that 68% of the population will be expected to achieve scores between 85 and 115 (see Figure 5.2).

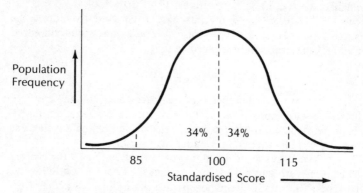

Figure 5.2   The distribution of scores on a standardised test.

This process is known as 'test standardisation' and the group of children on whom the test undergoes its trials are known as the 'standardisation sample'. Ideally this sample should be as large as possible and should draw on as wide a cross-section of society as is practicable. The sample should therefore attempt proportionately to represent different social and cultural groups, geographical location, etc.

Normative tests therefore enable comparisons to be made between the performance of an individual child and that *expected* from the population at large. The results will tell you how the child performed in relation to other children of similar age who were members of the standardised sample. They do not compare the child's performance with that of his immediate peer group either within the school or catchment area. Subsequent comparisons can be made between different children from a class or school in relation to their respective levels of performance on the test.

Examples of some of the normative tests frequently used in schools are shown in Table 5.2

Intelligence Tests

Of all the normative tests in regular use in recent years, intelligence tests (and the underlying concept of intelligence) have been the subject of more debate and controversy than any other (e.g. Kamin, 1974; Bolck and Dworkin, 1977; Simon, 1978, 1985; Eysenck and Kamin, 1981). The early development of such tests began in France after the turn of the century with the work of Alfred Binet. Cyril Burt played a major part in introducing them into the British education system. Their use was in keeping with the prevailing view about concepts of special education and the nature of children's learning. As was discussed in Chapter 2, 'intelligence' was seen as a crucial factor in accounting for children's different levels of academic achievement and so the practice of intelligence testing flourished.

When applied to children whose level of achievement was lower than that of their peers, it was thought that such tests could distinguish between:
— those children with a difficulty in learning reflected by a low level of intelligence, i.e they would be fulfilling their low potential and not expected to catch up with their peers,
— those children with higher levels of intelligence indicating that they were not fulfilling their potential; such children would be regarded as 'underachievers' and thus 'remediable'.

It is not the intention here to enter into the still continuing debate about the validity of 'intelligence' and intelligence tests. Further reading on the issue is suggested at the end of this Chapter. We would however make two points. The first is directly related to the general theme of this book: responding positively to special needs. Intelligence tests must therefore be subject to scrutiny in terms of how positively they contribute to the process of identifying and meeting children's educational needs. For example, how well do they bear comparison with curriculum-based and criterion-referenced testing in providing positive, actionable information which is to the educational benefit of the child? The second point relates to their being part of the normative test 'family'. Indeed it can be argued that the intelligence test is a more *generalised* measure of current attainments. In this sense, intelligence tests must also be subject to careful consideration of their composition and construction, their administration and the interpretation of the results they yield, especially when they form part of a school's testing practice.

Table 5.2
Some Normative Tests used in Schools

General abilities; Intelligence; Reasoning	Reading; Language	Mathematics; Arithmetic
Deeside Picture Test	Burt and Schonell Graded Word Reading Tests	APU Arithmetic Test
Moray House Verbal Reasoning Test	Edinburgh Reading Tests	Leicester Number Test
NFER Verbal Tests (BC, C, CD, D, EF, GH)	Gap Reading Comprehension Test	Moray House Mathematics Tests
NFER Non-Verbal Tests (BD, DH)	Gapadol Reading Comprehension Test	NFER Basic Mathematics Test (A, B, C, DE, FG)
NFER AH4 Group Test of General Intelligence	Holborn Reading Scale	NFER Mathematics Attainment Tests (A, B, C1/3, DE 1/2, EF)
Richmond Tests of Basic Skills	Neale Analysis of Reading Ability	Nottingham Number Test
Young: Oral Verbal Intelligence Test	NFER English Progress Tests (various)	Richmond Tests of Basic Skills
	NFER Reading Tests (AD, BD, DE, EH1–3)	Vernon: Grade Arithmetic-Mathematics Test.
	Richmond Tests of Basic Skills	
	Salford Sentence Reading Test	
	Southgate Group Reading Tests 1 and 2	
	SPAR Spelling and Reading Tests	
	Standard Reading Tests 1 and 12 (Daniels and Diack)	
	Widespan Reading Test	
	Young: Group Reading Test	

Child to parents: *Are these marks due to genetic or environmental factors?*

The Use of Normative Tests in Schools

The widespread use of normative tests in schools, including tests of intelligence and general ability, has rarely been the subject of detailed critical appraisal within LEAs. Administrators have often required the results of such tests to assist them in the overall evaluation of educational standards and in making decisions about the allocation of resources. In the preface to their comprehensive review of tests in use in the UK, Levy and Goldstein (1984) acknowledge that testing is a controversial activity and go on to state: 'part of this controversy is concerned with the way in which thoughtless or excessive use of tests can narrow or divert the educational curriculum.' To this we would add the danger that such tests, even where ostensibly appropriate, can be misapplied or misinterpreted to the detriment of children, not least those with special needs.

Teachers rarely undergo any specific training in the selection, use and interpretation of normative tests (Gipps, 1984). Potential users should bear in mind that the production of normative tests for use in schools has a commercial basis and that the caveat, *buyer beware,* is both appropriate and realistic. We therefore offer some cautionary guidelines.

Relevance.
— Why are you testing? What *practical* use will be made of the results; how and where will they be recorded; who will consult them; what is likely to happen next?
— Why has this particular test been selected? How appropriate is it to providing the information you want? Could you obtain the information you want in an alternative way (e.g. more easily, more directly)?
— How satisfactory is the test in terms of:
    recency of standardisation?
    adequacy of norms?
    adequacy of instructions?
    adequacy of information about reliability and validity?

Administration.
— Follow the instructions for administering the test accurately. If you do not, it would be questionable to record the test score. If you are unsure of the precise instructions, consult the test manual.
— Beware giving help except where permitted.
— Beware coaching or deliberately teaching to specific items contained in the test.
— Beware over-frequent use of test with the same pupils; this may lead to "practice effects" thereby reducing the validity of scores.

Rapport.
Establishing rapport with the child is essential. *You might* feel calm and relaxed, but how does the child feel? Particular attention should be paid to low-scoring children in order to ascertain other reasons for a poor level of performance (e.g. lack of concentration, anxiety, ill-health, misunderstanding of test instructions). If there are grounds for thinking that any of the above may have affected the child's performance, you should, at least *note this when recording his score* or not record a score at all.

Reliability.
Remember that *all* test scores are subject to *error* inherent in the test. Depending on the reliability of the test, this error usually amounts to as much as *plus/minus 5 points* of standardised score and sometimes as much as *plus/minus 10 points* .

Considerable caution is therefore required in assessing whether an observed score is a reliable indication of a child's performance on a particular test. This is especially true when looking for evidence of progress from one test occasion to another. What may *appear* to be progress, may be *test error.*

The test manual should state: (a) the reliability of the test and (b) how much error is likely to be associated with any *observed* score.

Validity.
What does your *observed score* mean:
— in relation to the type of test, the nature of its content?
— in relation to what has been taught?
— in relation to your original reason for using the test?

Recording test results.
In view of the above points, and the wide variation among tests, it is essential to record test results *fully*, so that appropriate interpretations can be made by any relevant professional (whether teacher, psychologist or adviser). The following should *always* be included:
— Precise name of test (just 'NFER' is insufficient; this agency produces many different kinds).
— Test score (state type, e.g. Standardised Score or Quotient; Percentile Rank; Test Age).
— Date administered.
— Age of child when tested.
— Any important qualifying comment (e.g. poor rapport).
— Tester's name.

Normative tests are not curriculum related although there may on occasions be a degree of overlap between skills included in the curriculum and skills sampled on the test. However, they are not sensitive to small gains made by a pupil in a given curriculum area. Furthermore they can usually only be administered at relatively long intervals which may mean only once or twice in the academic year and so do not readily fit into a view of assessment being a continuous process. They cannot therefore be used to monitor the progress of individual children on a day to day or week to week basis in the classroom.

Where they have been used in the past and could make a possible contribution within a school or LEA, is at the level of sampling performance levels of a *large* number of children. They can conceivably contribute to a general description of a group and help describe its characteristics and indentify *overall* needs. Using such tests in this way, as it were, to take a 'snapshot' of a group may help headteachers and administrators in decisions concerned with allocating resources, within the school and within the authority, respectively.

CRITERION-REFERENCED TESTS

Criterion-referenced tests are very different to normative tests. Unlike normative tests, they do not produce scores which enable comparisons to be made between pupils. In essence, they determine which skills in a given subject area a child has *learned* and by implication those that need to be taught in the future. They tell you what a pupil can do but do not provide information on how the pupil learns or how best to teach. They do not relate curriculum content and choice of teaching methods to a pupil's learning outcomes. They can therefore be useful in telling you what the child has achieved but not the conditions that most successfully facilitate the child's learning.

Criterion-referenced tests also have some of the limitations of normative tests. Those that are commercially available may not be sampling the content of the school's curriculum. Thus criterion-referenced tests need to be looked at carefully with respect to their validity. Are they testing the skills you wish them to test?

More positively, there are no constraints on how frequently criterion-referenced tests can be given. When their content closely reflects curriculum content, they can provide valuable information on a child's progress and the extent to which children are learning. However, because *published* criterion-reference tests usually only reflect the curriculum rather than *represent* it in detail, they cannot be given as often as might be desirable to give the necessary, regular feedback on children's progress. Table 5.3 presents some important differences between criterion-referenced tests and normative tests.

LOOKING AT INFORMATION FROM NORMATIVE AND CRITERION-REFERENCED TESTS

So what kind of picture of a child could be constructed following the administration of commercially available normative and criterion-referenced test? What will be known of his educational needs, the type of teaching environment he responds to, the teaching approaches most likely to facilitate future learning, the most suitable provision to meet his educational needs? Table 5.4 lists the test results of a child we will call James who had been experiencing difficulties in learning in his first year junior class. Let us assume that his behaviour, on occasions, was rather disruptive and this was also a cause of concern for his teacher.

In our illustration (Table 5.4) the actual tests used have not been named. We wish to focus on the information they provide and see how that helps in answering the above questions and relates to the guidelines for assessment presented in Circular 1/83.

Table 5.4 does not contain an exhaustive list of all the possible normative and criterion-referenced tests that could be given under these circumstances. However, they illustrate the kind of information available and how it can be interpreted.

On normative tests, the average standardised score is 100. A score of anything less than 100 is therefore considered to be 'below average' in relation to children of a comparable age, and anything higher, 'above average'. James' results indicate that he is below average in reading and arithmetic, average in expressive and receptive language and of above

Table 5.3
Some Important Differences Between Criterion-referenced Tests and Normative Tests

Criterion-referenced tests	Normative tests
Concerned solely with an individual pupil's performance on a specific 'criterion' task.	Concerned with comparing performance of pupil in some 'ability' area with that of peer group (children of similar age).
Derived from the teaching objectives set by teacher; directly related to curriculum.	Derived from the hypothetical notion of 'ability' determined by test constructor; not directly related to curriculum.
Gives explicit information on what pupil can and cannot do; what he needs to be taught.	Few teaching implications.
Can be undertaken in normal teaching situation (i.e. classroom)	Undertaken in medical room, interview room, headteacher's study, etc. or in group situation under 'exam' conditions.
Can be administered by regular classteachers with relatively little training.	Should be administered by psychologist/teacher who is thoroughly familiar with test manual and procedures.
May be repeated frequently (e.g. on day-to-day, week-to-week basis).	Can only be given infrequently (e.g. yearly) otherwise problems of practice effect.
Provide basis for continuous monitoring of pupil's performance in school, keeping records, etc.	Often used in making placement decisions (e.g. for special schooling) or in surveys of educational achievement for research purposes.
Does not involve 'labelling'; pupil's *performance* is described not the pupil himself.	Risk of pupil being labelled as 'low IQ', 'dull', 'retarded reader', etc.
Tests can be very brief.	Tests usually time-consuming.
Tests can be prepared by the teacher; some are published commercially	Published test materials needed; some tests 'restricted' (i.e. not available to teachers).

Table 5.4
Some Normative and Criterion-referenced Test Results on an Individual Pupil

Child's Name: James
Age: 8 years 2 months

Test	Type	Result
Reading	Normative	Reading Age: 6 years 2 months
Arithmetic	Normative	Standardised Score: 75
Language	Normative	Receptive Language Standardised Score: 97
		Expressive Language Standardised Score: 102
Intelligence test	Normative	IQ: 100
Reading	Criterion-referenced	Can name some letters sounds
		Cannot blend 3 letter words (e.g. cat, sit, pod)
		Sight vocabulary of 15 words
Reading Comprehension	Normative	Standardised Score: 82
Arithmetic	Criterion-referenced	Can add numbers where answers do not exceed 20
		Can subtract numbers up to 10
		Cannot multiply or divide
		Can name coins but not add, subtract, etc. with money
		Can tell time on digital watch but not using a clock face
Behaviour	Checklist	Disruptive, socially withdrawn

average intelligence. The criterion-referenced tests show some of the skills that he has learned and those that still need to be taught. Finally the conclusions to be drawn from completing the behaviour checklist suggest that he is disruptive and withdrawn.

The first issue that needs to be considered is the group of children with whom James is being compared. Each of the five normative tests has been standardised on a *different group of children*. Therefore how James has performed on each of these tests is being related to five groups of pupils whose composition may vary greatly. Is it valid to conclude that because he is above average in IQ, average in expressive language and receptive language and below average in reading and arithmetic, he has a problem in these latter two subjects? Will it not depend on the children who comprise these groups as much as James' skills in the areas being investigated?

For example, one way to look at the results of this kind of information is to think of how English athletes perform in events such as the Commonwealth, European and Olympic games. English athletes always compare favourably with their Commonwealth counterparts and win a large number of medals. Fewer medals are won in the European Championships, and the combined forces of England, Scotland, Wales and Northern Ireland win fewer still when performing on the world stage at the Olympic Games. The athlete who is above average in Commonwealth competition is frequently below average at Olympic level. There are clearly dangers in drawing too many conclusions about an athlete's competence until we know whom he is being compared with. The same can be said about a child completing a series of normative tests. The test results must be viewed in relation to the make up of the standardised group.

Even more importantly though, when a child likes James performs at a level which is below average on tests such as the reading and arithmetic ones, we do not know how he compares to his *immediate* peer group, that is to say children in his own school or catchment area. James has been assessed in isolation. It may be that if these children had taken the same test as James, they would not have performed as well as him. So even though he was below average when compared to the standardisation sample in reading and arithmetic, his immediate peers might have also performed at a level well below average.

There are therefore a number of dangers when focusing on a single child and trying to assess his educational needs by the use of normative tests. It is important to be clear about the groups of children with whom comparisons are being made. Is it a standardisation sample or the child's immediate peer group? Which groups do you actually want to make comparisons with? In which aspects of a child's level of school performance do you wish to make comparisons?

The criterion-referenced tests reveal some of the skills James has learned. However, they convey little information regarding *how* learning took place. When given on a single occasion like a 'snapshot' there is no way of knowing *how long* it took James to learn the skills tested. They also give no indication of the *patterns of classroom organisation* and *teaching methods* that have been most successful in facilitating James' learning.

What is learned about a child's attainment levels similarly depends on the criterion-referenced tests given to the pupil. Their content varies and they may be giving information on performance levels in areas which are not immediately relevant when assessing the educational needs of the child in question.

Finally there is the behaviour checklist. It shares many of the limitations of normative and criterion-referenced tests, since it serves to *summarise* people's perceptions of the child's behaviour. In general it does not take into account the total environment in which a child exists and interacts. Similarly labelling the child's behaviour as disruptive and withdrawn does not convey any indication of James' educational needs. What skills does he need to be taught? What is the most appropriate provision to meet those needs?

To summarise, our illustration of James' assessment enables tentative conclusions to be drawn about:

— his performance levels in relation to the *particular normative tests used,*
— some of the basic academic skills that he has learned,
— a *label* to describe his behaviour.

The main criticism of this form of assessment is the fact that it can only be carried out infrequently, on a single occasion. It also assumes that the pupil is not overawed by the test situation and is able to perform at an optimal level. Although we have higlighted a number of criticisms of this type of assessment they could be overcome, to some extent, by considering the issues outlined in this chapter.

Equally important though, is how this approach to assessment compares with the exhortations of Circular 1/83. Here, assessment is seen as a *continuous* process, which looks at the child's *strengths* and *weaknesses*, considers the way he *interacts with his environment*, and is *related to teaching*. In this context, different strategies are tried out to find out how the child responds best. There is no doubt, in our view that this orientation would ultimately lead to a more comprehensive understanding of the child's needs and the most suitable, subsequent provision. A crucial feature of this view of continuous assessment is the need to keep high quality records so that different approaches are noted and closely related to the child's learning. Teachers are encouraged to follow this course of action in Circular 1/83 (Paragraph 11).

Normative tests are clearly not the natural components of such an approach to assessment. They are *not* continuous, *not* directly related to day-to-day teaching *nor* experimental in nature. Criterion-referenced tests, whilst having a number of positive features, also have some limitations. They can lead to an undue focus on a child's weaknesses rather than his strengths and may, at worst, lead to a catalogue of deficits. Finally, as they are not usually derived from the curricula used in school, they can rarely give the necessary feedback on a child's day-to-day progress.

SUMMARY

The concept of assessment as conveyed in Circular 1/83 is more in keeping with current trends in special education as referred to in Chapter 2. Even outside the arena of special education, there have been significant moves away from assessment and selection procedures based purely on the administration of standardised tests. The new GCSE examinations and emphasis on pupil profiling are, in principle, attempts to obtain a more complete picture of children's learning over a period of time and in response to different situations.

What emerges from Circular 1/83 is that assessment is a process which should form part of everyday teaching rather than being distinct and separate from it. This should apply, whatever theory of learning the practitioner adheres to. Although this has been stated earlier in the book we think it worthy of emphasis. Irrespective of the perceived cause of a child's difficulty, an inescapable conclusion is that attempts must be made ultimately to provide the child with the skills and learning experiences he lacks. It is only after exposing a child to systematic teaching, where different teaching approaches and patterns of classroom organisation are tried, evaluated and related to the child's learning, that we will gain practical insights into the child's educational needs. This must now be viewed as an integral feature of the assessment process.

FURTHER READING

Gillham, B. ed. (1978). *Reconstructing Educational Psychology,* Croom Helm, London.
> A collection of chapters taking a critical look at the present status and future trends of educational psychology. A particularly relevant chapter on test usage entitled 'The Failure of Psychometrics'.

Gipps, C. (1984). Issues in the use of standardised tests by teachers. *Bulletin of the British Psychological Society* **37,** 135-156.
> Discusses the results of a survey into teachers' use and interpretation of normative tests in primary and secondary schools.

Howell, K., Kaplan, J. and O'Connell, C. (1979). *Evaluating Exceptional Children : a Task Analysis Approach,* Chas. E. Merrill, Columbus, Ohio.
> A good American source book on approaches to children with special needs. Useful early chapters on issues relating to assessment and the use of IQ, attainment and diagnostic tests.

Levy, P. and Goldstein, H. (1984). *Tests in Education : a Book of Critical Reviews,* Academic Press, London.

Does he have a mental block?
Is it his low IQ?
Perhaps he has a specific learning difficulty?
Maybe it's his home background?

Am I choosing tasks at the right level of difficulty?
Am I making the task interesting?
Is there a more effective teaching method I could try?
Do I praise him enough?

Seeking Explanations for Educational Failure.

A comprehensive and authoritative text providing detailed reviews of a wide range of ability, attainment and diagnostic tests used in the UK.

Swann, W. (1982). *Unit 12: Psychology and Special Education.* (Course E241: Special Needs in Education), Open University Press, Milton Keynes.
Chapter 2 provides a critical view of the use of IQ tests in special education.

Vincent, D., Green, L., Francis, J. and Powney, J. (1983). *A Review of Reading Tests*, NFER – Nelson, Windsor.
Critical reviews of several tests and assessment procedures in reading and related skills for use in British schools.

Chapter Six

ASSESSMENT-THROUGH-TEACHING

The purpose of an assessment carried out under the Education Act 1981 is to establish what a child's educational needs are and what provision is considered appropriate to meet those needs. Through the discussions in Chapters 4 and 5 it has been possible to convey a flavour of the requirements of an effective assessment procedure. Assessment should be seen as a process taking place over a period of time which is closely related to education, with the school and in particular the class teacher taking a central role. Assessment is also a collaborative venture between a school, a child's parents or guardian and other professionals from outside agencies.

Behind the statement, 'I think child X has a difficulty in learning', lies an assumption that frequently remains *unstated*. The assumption is that the teaching offered and learning environment provided could not, as far as we are aware, have been improved upon given existing provision. Obviously if they could, steps would have been taken to do something to bring about the necessary changes.

Teachers are now in the position of having to demonstrate this within the context of the Education Act. Both the parents and the LEA will want to see and be satisfied that no more could have been done to facilitate the child's learning under existing circumstances, and that additional provision now needs to be considered. There is therefore a need for detailed records that can be used as an integral part of the teaching process to help inform decision making and yet at the same time provide a comprehensive account of teaching approaches tried in relation to the respective learning outcomes for the child.

Any approach to assessment has to meet several criteria. It must, as has been mentioned, be continuous and ultimately lead to a greater appreciation of the child's educational needs, whether they be designated special or otherwise. However, it is not entirely clear from the Education Act precisely what a special need is.

In the Act itself, a special educational need is defined in relation to whether a child requires special educational provision to be made for him. Whether special educational provision is required will depend on whether the child has a learning difficulty which is 'significantly greater than the majority of children of his age' and/or 'has a disability which either prevents or hinders him from making use of educational facilities of a kind generally provided in schools, within the area of the local authority concerned, for children of his age' (Section 1, Subsection 2).

Unfortunately this definition of special educational needs does not specify *what* an educational need is. The Act states *when* a child has a special educational need, i.e. that he has a learning difficulty significantly greater ... etc. and that this should result in special educational provision being made available. But how do we know whether a child has a learning difficulty and how does this relate to specifying a pupil's educational needs? The process of assessment must therefore articulate a pupil's educational needs and provide a framework for determining whether the child has a learning difficulty, so a decision can be taken about the necessity of additional provision.

The assessment process must also be compatible with any theory of learning held by the teachers or professionals coming into contact with a child. Many reasons have been advanced to account for why children experience difficulties in school. They vary in the range of contributory factors identified and how best to respond to them. However, Circular 1/83 offers sufficient guidelines from which to infer the salient characteristics of an acceptable approach to assessment, which can accommodate theoretical differences in explanations of causality. Table 6.1 summarises the functions of the assessment process.

Table 6.1
Functions of the Assessment Process

The assessment process must:
Lead to the identification of the child's educational needs.
Demonstrate what can be achieved with existing provision.
Indicate whether the child has a difficulty in learning which is significantly greater than the majority of children of his age.
Contribute to a formulation of appropriate provision to meet the child's needs.

We now proceed to offer a broader model of assessment which is gaining ground in special education both in the USA (Blankenship and Lilly, 1981) and in the UK (Pearson and Tweddle, 1984; Raybould, 1984; Solity and Bull, 1987), and is fully compatible with the concepts of assessment offered by the DES. The model recognises the inter-relationship of planning, teaching, learning and evaluation.

Before describing the assessment-through-teaching model, a word needs to be said about its principal focus of concern. It concentrates on the classroom environment, in particular the teaching arrangements and patterns of organisation adopted to promote children's learning. Its emphasis is on factors which a teacher can influence *directly*. To this extent it does not address itself to a child's home background.

Clearly a child's family and life experiences have a major bearing on how she deals with the learning and social demands of school. However, the processes which influence a child's development are complex. No matter how we try, our understanding and appreciation of the effects of a child's personal life will always be incomplete and will be affected by a number of issues, some of which are discussed in Chapter 9, Working with Parents.

The new legislation requires teachers to make an assessment of a child's *educational needs*. It is expected that other parties will comment on alternative, relevant aspects of the child's life. So whilst acknowledging the impact of home factors, the exclusive emphasis in this chapter is on the classroom environment, and its influence on children's learning.

ASSESSMENT-THROUGH-TEACHING AND CHILDREN PRESENTING LEARNING DIFFICULTIES

The basic model of continuous assessment which we are advocating was originated by Robert Glaser in the early 1960s and has since been developed and applied in a variety of special educational settings, both in the USA and UK. The essential principle is that assessment and teaching are inextricably related. Without assessment there can be no adequate teaching and without teaching, there can be no adequate assessment. This inter-relationship is represented in Table 6.2. We shall now describe the components of this approach.

Determine the Curriculum Sequence

The first component is to have an overall plan of the skills you want to teach the pupil and the broad sequence in which you want to teach them. Ultimately what do you want the child to be able to *do?* What activities should the pupil be able to complete and what skills are required to perform those activities? To set clear goals gives the day-to-day work with a child experiencing difficulties a broader perspective and helps the teacher maintain a sense of direction and purpose. Setting targets in this way can also be highly motivating for the child.

The skills to be taught should where possible be placed in a logical sequence so that teaching earlier skills facilitates the learning of the later and possibly more complex ones. This will make it easier for the child to progress through the sequence and reach stated goals.

For some, the notion that the curriculum can be organised into a logical sequence of skills and concepts for children to learn may well be an anathema. To do so is frequently seen as narrowing children's learning experiences and therefore restricting their overall development.

However, where this view is held, it is important to recognise the crucial distinction between *what* and *how* children learn. *How* a child learns and the experiences that are deemed most likely to promote

Table 6.2
The Basic Model of Assessment-Through-Teaching

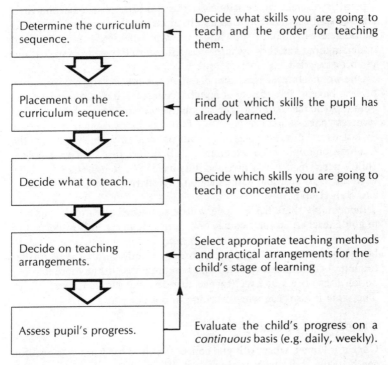

Determine the curriculum sequence.	Decide what skills you are going to teach and the order for teaching them.
Placement on the curriculum sequence.	Find out which skills the pupil has already learned.
Decide what to teach.	Decide which skills you are going to teach or concentrate on.
Decide on teaching arrangements.	Select appropriate teaching methods and practical arrangements for the child's stage of learning
Assess pupil's progress.	Evaluate the child's progress on a *continuous* basis (e.g. daily, weekly).

learning are, within this model, dealt with under the fourth component, i.e. deciding on the teaching arrangements. These are essentially determined by the teacher and will therefore be consistent with *the teacher's own view* of how children learn.

At the same time, to espouse a particular view of how children learn also carries with it a responsibility to specify some of the key learning outcomes. It might not always be possible to identify these within a logical sequence, but it is reasonable to expect, in our view, that a teacher should articulate these outcomes. Again, to do so does not in any way preclude the teacher from *observing and encouraging learning that had not been specified in advance,* but at the very least ensures a child's progress is continually being monitored and evaluated in relation to what is deemed necessary and desirable for him to learn.

Placement on the Curriculum

The next component once the overall sequence of skills has been determined, is to find out which skills have already been learned by the child so the pupil can be placed accurately on the curriculum sequence.

This usually involves devising a number of graded activities which correspond to the identified skills. The activities are given in turn until a point is reached where it is clear the child has passed beyond their level of skill acquisition. It should then be possible to state with some confidence which skills the child uses with complete competence and understanding and those where such a standard of performance has not yet been reached.

One implication of this component in the assessment process is the need to have a clear idea of acceptable criteria to indicate that learning of any particular skill has been adequately demonstrated. This is often seen as one of education's $64 000 questions which applies to mainstream education generally but is crucially important in the teaching of pupils who experience difficulties. Just how well does a child's performance on a given activity have to be to indicate it has been well and truly learned? Guidance on this matter is to found in Solity and Bull (1987).

Lamentably there has been very little published research in this area to guide teachers in their choice of criteria. However, it is important to bear in mind that when a child is learning any new skill, a point has to be reached where the pupil can use that skill without any further teaching being necessary. This aim is represented in the more familiar notion that once you have learned to ride a bicycle you never forget. The same is also true when learning important educational skills.

Decide What to Teach

Once it is known what skills and concepts a child has learned, a decision can be taken about what to teach next. Where the curriculum sequence can be arranged in a logical manner, learning earlier skills should facilitate the acquisition of later and possibly more complex ones. The overall aim is to select tasks and activities which are at an appropriate level of difficulty and which provide opportunities for future success.

We have outlined a model whereby certain skills and concepts will be identified *within* particular curriculum areas, but it should be recognised that in some instances these skills and concepts will be relevant *across* curriculum boundaries. Where this is so, children should be encouraged to develop their knowledge and newly acquired skills as broadly as possible.

Choice of Teaching Arrangements

The fourth component in the process focuses on the selection of suitable teaching methods, materials and patterns of classroom organisation. This is the area that initially seems most daunting to class teachers when working with children experiencing difficulties.

First of all, a common expectation might be that it is going to be time consuming since it is felt the children will need individual attention and teaching on a one-to-one basis. How can sufficient time be found in a typically busy school day to provide the help required?

A second possible cause of concern and potential source of frustration when planning a programme to help a particular child, is the starting position. We begin with the knowledge that they have not learned from our best efforts to date. The teaching methods that worked with other children have not succeeded with them.

It is useful to look at these issues in the light of a hierarchy of instructional approaches proposed by Haring and Eaton (1978) (Table 6.3). The hierarchy contains five stages, each one corresponding to a level of learning to be achieved by the child. It is called an instructional hierarchy because of its emphasis on ways of organising aspects of the teaching environment to promote the five stages of learning.

Table 6.3
The Instructional Hierarchy

Aquisition	Children are shown how to use a skill for the first time and learn to perform it *accurately*.
Fluency	Children learn to perform the new skill with *fluency* as well as *accuracy*.
Maintenance	Children are still able to perform the skill accurately and fluently even after a period of time when no direct teaching has taken place on that skill. Opportunities are created for continued skill usage.
Generalisation	Children are shown how to use the skill in different contexts.
Adaptation	Children are set problems which require them to apply their newly acquired skills or knowledge independently.

During the acquisition stage, the child is introduced to a new task for the first time. The aim of teaching at this stage is for the child to perform new skills to a high level of accuracy. It is likely that at some point during teaching, a relatively high level of pupil–teacher interaction will be required as the child is shown how to use the new skill.

Accuracy provides the platform from which to develop fluency. During the fluency stage, the child will need practice so that using the skill becomes 'second nature'. It is best if he works independently during this stage and gets as many opportunities as possible to use the new skill. This is a stage of teaching that is often under-emphasised or omitted from the learning experiences of children with difficulties. It can be tempting to move a child on to a new task once *accuracy alone* has been achieved, through a desire to speed up children's progress through the curriculum. Yet if the child is denied the opportunity to develop fluency, it is likely he will forget what he has learned and before long the teacher will be back at square one (trying to build accuracy again).

Over time, it is important that children maintain their levels of performance without any further teaching taking place. During the maintenance stage, therefore, periodic checks are made to ensure they can still perform previously learned skills to stated criterial levels. At the end of the stage children should be able to complete tasks on their own, with accuracy and fluency but without receiving any direct input from the teacher. It would also be expected that children would now be finding tasks increasingly rewarding in their own right as a result of experiencing progress.

These first three stages of the hierarchy concentrate on *skill-getting*. The last two stages, generalisation and adaptation, represent a change in emphasis to *skill-using*. During generalisation, children are taught to use the skills they have learned, in a range of new contexts. The aim is to illustrate how skills can be applied so that children are then in a position to generalise their knowledge. The teacher takes an active role during this stage, demonstrating the principles underlying the process of generalisation and arranging opportunities for application.

The fifth stage, adaptation, is often best thought of as children offering 'creative' solutions to posed questions and problems. They extend their skills and respond in novel ways through synthesising newly acquired skills with existing knowledge. As with the stages of fluency and maintenance, there is little direct teacher involvement during adaptation. The teacher is merely 'on hand' to answer queries, check on progress and provide feedback and general encouragement.

The instructional hierarchy can usefully be related to the stages that many of us go through when learning something new. Think of learning to drive a car and the steady progression through comparable levels of development, from nervous beginner to competent driver. Alternatively, note how a musician learns a new piece of music. Initially after becoming accurate and fluent the work can be memorised and subjected to a range of different stylistic interpretations. Success in the later, more creative stages, is dependent on a sure command of the prerequisite stages. And so it is with teaching children important academic skills.

The instructional hierarchy is helpful in several ways. It serves to remind us what it is hoped will be achieved when teaching children with difficulties. The ultimate aim is to enable them to reach a level where they can generalise and apply their knowledge adaptively and independently.

Secondly, guidelines are suggested for organising the teaching approach. The hierarchy provides a framework into which existing classroom practice can be incorporated to ensure children's smooth transition from accuracy and fluency through to generalisation and adaptation. To view teaching in this way will be helpful when planning which methods to use and relating this to children's learning outcomes. (For guidance on how this may be achieved see Solity, 1988; Solity and Bull, 1987.)

During the assessment process, it is not necessarily a matter of trying to find new approaches to teaching but implementing existing ones at the appropriate, critical time to promote specific stages of learning. It is unlikely that any single strategy will be successful in enabling children to attain all the levels of learning specified in the hierarchy.

Changes in teacher involvement occur in several ways as skills are taught at different stages. Teachers initially take an active role in the teaching process (acquisition stage) but subsequently become facilitators, providing the appropriate environment in which a pupil's skill development can flourish. So contrary to common expectations, much of children's learning can involve them working independently. Only a relatively small part of teaching will require either one-to-one pupil–teacher involvement or direct, small group teaching.

Assess Pupil's Progress

In the fifth and final component of the model, children's progress is evaluated and related to the previous components, choice of curriculum, placement on the curriculum, selection of skills and teaching arrangements. The types of questions asked would frequently be along the following lines:

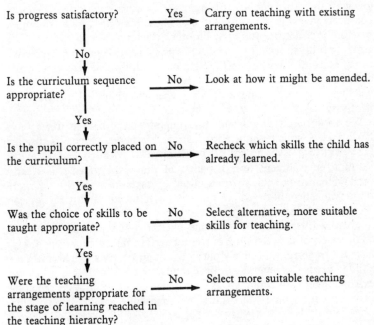

Is progress satisfactory?   **Yes**   Carry on teaching with existing arrangements.

    No

Is the curriculum sequence appropriate?   **No**   Look at how it might be amended.

    Yes

Is the pupil correctly placed on the curriculum?   **No**   Recheck which skills the child has already learned.

    Yes

Was the choice of skills to be taught appropriate?   **No**   Select alternative, more suitable skills for teaching.

    Yes

Were the teaching arrangements appropriate for the stage of learning reached in the teaching hierarchy?   **No**   Select more suitable teaching arrangements.

Assessment-through-teaching is a process which attempts to identify those aspects of the classroom environment which most effectively promote a child's learning.

The instructional hierarchy is especially important in this respect. It facilitates a much more comprehensive understanding of a child's needs through linking specific teaching approaches to stages of learning. Where a child is having difficulties but is appropriately placed on the curriculum, we can focus on each level of the hierarchy and see whether the problem arises at the acquisition, fluency, maintenance, generalisation or adaptation stages. We might then discover that a child can reach maintenance quickly but needs special attention when developing generalisation.

The evaluation component helps considerably in making a detailed analysis of the child's educational needs. It is possible to find out precisely what the pupil can already do and what skills need to be taught next. Because the curriculum content is constantly under review it can be revised and adapted when necessary to give a full appreciation of a pupil's needs.

The assessment-through-teaching model also enables recommendations to be made about the most suitable form of provision to meet the child's needs. Finding time to teach a child experiencing difficulties is always a major concern for the busy class teacher. The purpose of the continuous assessment period is to make the best possible use of *existing resources and provision*. In effect this involves providing the planning and teaching time that is feasible and realistic given all the other demands being made on a teacher's time. It should not be seen as an occasion for offering *extra help* which impinges, possibly in a detrimental way, on other teaching responsibilities. The aim is to find out what progress a child is able to make with the effective use of current provision. In the light of this, informed decisions, based on continuous records, can be taken about what the child's needs are, whether they are being met and whether additional provision is necessary.

We appreciate that assessment-through-teaching may at times seem like an ideal which is not always attainable under school conditions. However, to present a view of the child based on his responses to the learning environment over a period of time ('the video'), is clearly preferable, in our view, to a form of assessment which is more impressionistic and based on information gathered on only one or two occasions ('the snapshot').

There will however, be occasions when it is only possible to provide an overview of how a child is currently performing. We may not always have the opportunities to 'try out different approaches to help meet the child's needs' as suggested in Circular 1/83 (Paragraph 11). For example, there are circumstances under which advice may be called for urgently, in which case only 'a snapshot' would be possible.

Nonetheless, even when circumstances limit the extent of the assessment, we would argue that the snapshot should be in focus and might also include an accurate 'action-replay' of what has been learned about the child's educational needs from previous attempts to teach him.

ASSESSMENT-THROUGH-TEACHING AND CHILDREN PRESENTING BEHAVIOUR PROBLEMS

Thus far, the model of assessment-through-teaching has been described in relation to children who present learning difficulties. It is equally valid, particularly within the terms of reference of the Education Act, when applied to children whose social behaviour is a cause for concern. The aim of assessment remains the same, to establish the child's needs and most suitable provision to meet those needs, while at the same time recording and evaluating the impact of existing resources. The assessment-through-teaching model when applied to children's behaviour is presented in Table 6.4.

The starting point in the assessment process is to identify both the long-term goals and more immediate targets for children's social development. How are they expected to behave inside and outside the classroom, what is regarded as acceptable behaviour in the school, what patterns of social interactions are to be encouraged? It is useful to think of this as developing a 'curriculum for social behaviour', very much for the same reasons as it is essential to have a curriculum for skills to be taught.

The 'behavioural curriculum' is a backdrop against which to view a child's behaviour, and would be the equivalent of the first component of the assessment-through-teaching model. An analysis of the child's current behaviour, based on systematic observation by those school staff coming into contact with the pupil is essential for pinpointing those aspects of his social behaviour which are considered satisfactory and those that are not. In what ways is the pupil's behaviour already acceptable and consistent with the goals stated in the behavioural curriculum? It is rarely helpful to dwell for too long on what the child is doing wrong. Instead attention should turn to those patterns of social behaviour it is hoped the pupil will learn.

Nevertheless it is not always easy to draw a line between unwanted behaviour that is just 'annoying' and that which can be properly described as a 'problem'. No one wants to over-react to occasional misbehaviour or exacerbate behaviour which might remit, without intervention anyway. Leach and Raybould (1977) and Bull and Solity (1987) outline a number of steps which can assist in making judgements about the seriousness of a child's unwanted behaviour.

Initially it is important for a teacher to think about her own reaction to a child's behaviour and be clear that it is the behaviour that is the

Table 6.4
Assessment-Through-Teaching and Children's Social Behaviour

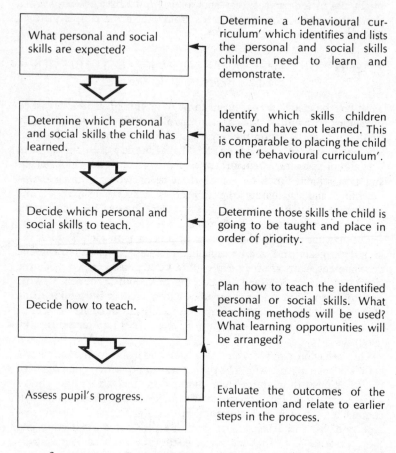

What personal and social skills are expected?	Determine a 'behavioural curriculum' which identifies and lists the personal and social skills children need to learn and demonstrate.
Determine which personal and social skills the child has learned.	Identify which skills children have, and have not learned. This is comparable to placing the child on the 'behavioural curriculum'.
Decide which personal and social skills to teach.	Determine those skills the child is going to be taught and place in order of priority.
Decide how to teach.	Plan how to teach the identified personal or social skills. What teaching methods will be used? What learning opportunities will be arranged?
Assess pupil's progress.	Evaluate the outcomes of the intervention and relate to earlier steps in the process.

cause for concern and not the pupil. Sometimes, especially if a pupil is proving particularly troublesome, it is not easy to remain totally objective and disentangle personal feelings and reactions to a child from a detached view of the behaviour displayed.

Next an attempt must be made to try and define exactly what the child is doing that is disruptive. Rather than describe the child's behaviour as, for example, 'aggressive', 'withdrawn' or 'disruptive', etc., it is helpful to be more specific and identify the actual actions which are aggressive or withdrawn. The assessment-through-teaching model urges that a distinction is made between what the child *is* (i.e. 'disruptive', 'aggressive', etc.) and what the child *does* (i.e. 'hits other children', 'calls out', etc.). When pinpointing children's unacceptable behaviour and trying to identify what should be taught next, it is best to focus on what the child *does,* and not what it is thought he *is.* For example, it is possible to make it clear to a child that you still like her, even though you may disapprove of aspects of her behaviour.

After noting what the child does, the extent of the problem can be most fully appreciated by observing the pupil in the full range of school settings. In a secondary school this would clearly need to be well co-ordinated and involve all the staff coming into contact with the pupil. The *frequency, duration* and *reasonableness* of the behaviour together with the *settings* in which it occurs and the extent to which it interferes with, or disrupts the child's *own* development (academically and socially) should all be recorded over a period of time in order to gauge the seriousness of the unwanted behaviour.

A child's behaviour also needs to be related to his peer group in three ways. How do other children in the class, or of a similar age, in the school behave? To what degree does the child's behaviour stand out as being different from that of his peers? Secondly to what extent does the unwanted behaviour interrupt or interfere with the activitites of peers, either inside or outside the classroom? Finally how do other children respond to the behaviour of the pupil who is misbehaving? Do they relate positively or negatively to the child? Is he an accepted member of the peer group or not?

These issues enable a teacher or school staff to clarify *how problematic* the behaviour is. Does it warrant some form of ameliorative intervention or is it a one-off event that is underpinned by specific factors which are not likely to persist? The steps outlined are summarised in Table 6.5.

Table 6.5
Steps in Estimating the Seriousness of Unwanted Behaviour

Step 1	The teacher examines her own reactions to both the child and his behaviour.
Step 2	Pinpoint precisely what the child is *doing* that is a cause for concern.
Step 3	Observe the unwanted behaviour(s), noting: — frequency, — duration, — the settings in which it occurs (i.e. how generalised or situation-specific it is), — the extent to which it interferes with or disrupts the child's *own* development (academically and socially).
Step 4	Relate the child's unwanted behaviour to that of his peers in terms of: — the expected behaviour for children of a similar age, in similar circumstances, — the extent to which the unwanted behaviour interrupts or interferes with peers, — how peers respond.

After identifying the skills already acquired by the pupil from the behavioural curriculum, a decision has to be taken about what to teach next. For every unacceptable behaviour there is nearly always a positive alternative. If a child 'calls out' in class the acceptable alternative might be to raise a hand to seek the teacher's attention and permission before speaking. If a pupil is 'always' out of her seat, a more appropriate pattern of classroom behaviour would be for the pupil to remain in her seat. It is these positive alternatives that become the subsequent teaching targets of the planned intervention.

The fourth component is to select a pattern of classroom organisation and teaching approaches to try and teach the pupil the acceptable alternative. Again the aim here is to do the best with existing resources, devoting only as much time and attention as is reasonable given the other responsibilities to be undertaken. The purpose of the continuous assessment is to establish how far the child's needs are currently met and what additional provision might be necessary if they are not. Finally, the fifth component of the assessment-through-teaching model would require the intervention to be carefully evaluated, the child's progress being related to the previous steps in the assessment process (i.e. what has been tried out with what outcome).

TWO VIEWS OF ASSESSMENT

There are two kinds of 'assessment' within the assessment-through-teaching model. The second component in the process, curriculum placement, is concerned with finding out what a child has already learned and deciding what to teach next. Here an 'assessment' is being made of the child's current skill levels. This then leads to the identification of future educational needs.

The fifth component represents another kind of assessment. It refers to the assessment of the child's learning outcomes, made in response to the choice of teaching approaches and arrangement of the classroom environment. Assessment here attempts to pinpoint those features of the way a child is taught which are instrumental in promoting learning.

The assessment of educational needs concentrates on the child, identifying his current achievements. It does not attempt to explain what factors might have given rise to them. It is simply a statement of what the child has already learned.

The second view of assessment is concerned with the child's interaction with his environment and how he responds to different situations. The question to which an answer is sought is, 'What factors give rise to successful learning experiences for the child?'

THE TEACHER AND ASSESSMENT-THROUGH-TEACHING

The teacher takes a major role in carrying out an assessment-through-teaching. The assessment is classroom-based and 'experimental' in orientation. Different teaching approaches and patterns of classroom organisation are used to estimate their impact on children's learning. The overall aim of the assessment is to establish the child's educational needs in the light of *what has been tried* and evaluate the extent to which the needs can be met by existing provision.

The assessment can be viewed as a feasibility study, trying to see whether what the school is able to offer is going to be suitable to meet the child's needs. Inevitably, where it is felt those needs are not being met, there will be a tendency for those teaching the child to feel they have 'failed' through not being able to promote the child's learning or development to a level for which they had hoped. Such feelings need to be put in perspective and set alongside the knowledge and understanding that would have been gained about the child's needs. 'Success' within assessment-through-teaching is related to the functions of assessment and whether:

— the child's needs have been identified,
— the adequacy of existing provision has been shown,
— it has been *demonstrated* whether a child has a difficulty in learning,
— appropriate provision to meet the child's needs can be formulated.

The fact that a pupil has not met the teacher's expectations for his rate of progress and attainment levels should not in itself give rise to negative perceptions, if the main functions of the assessment have been achieved.

THE EDUCATION ACT AND ASSESSMENT-THROUGH-TEACHING

The main principles of assessment, advanced in Circular 1/83 and described in Chapter 3 can be summarised as follows:

— the focus is on the child rather than his disability and should identify not only his strengths and weaknesses but also his personal resources and attributes, together with the nature of his interaction with his environment,
— be a means of arriving at a better understanding of the child's learning difficulties for the practical purpose of providing a guide to his education and a basis against which to monitor his progress,
— be a continuous process,
— be a partnership between teachers, other professionals and parents in a joint endeavour to discover and understand the nature of the difficulties and needs of individual children,
— always be closely related to education.

These principles are also at the heart of the continuous assessment model represented by assessment-through-teaching. The individual child together with his interaction with the learning environment is the focus of attention. The pupil is looked at very much in terms of what he can already do (his strengths) which provides the platform for future teaching. By concentrating on a child's positive achievements the temptation to label a child through trying to describe a disability is avoided. The assessment emphasis is very firmly on what the child does and needs, not what he is.

The process takes place in the classroom, the child's most familiar environment and is closely related to education. It fits readily into existing classroom practice and through its experimental nature ultimately offers guidance on appropriate forms of provision to meet a child's needs.

Assessment-through-teaching facilitates the partnership between teachers, professionals and parents. Its aims can be clearly articulated and parents can see the efforts made to maximise the effectiveness of existing resources as a means of finding out what is best to meet their child's educational needs. Detailed records are kept for each step in the assessment process which provide the basis for discussion with those coming into contact with the child and help make the partnership a productive and open collaboration.

RECORD KEEPING AND ASSESSMENT-THROUGH-TEACHING

Fundamental to assessment-through-teaching is an effective record keeping system. This lies at the core of both planning continuous, systematic, experimental teaching and informed discussion with parents, other professionals and colleagues. Table 6.6 summarises the reasons for developing and maintaining curriculum-based records when assessing the educational needs of children experiencing difficulties.

Records facilitate each component in the process documenting what the child can already do and indicating what is to be taught next. Through detailing the effects of existing teaching approaches on children's learning, the appropriateness of current provision can be ascertained, together with likely amendments and additions.

Detailed, up-to-date records are also essential when a school is preparing reports for the LEA about their observations on a child derived from the period of assessment. Their relevance in this context will be discussed in Chapter 7. However, we would stress the importance of records when representing the substance of the assessment-through-teaching process to the outside world, whether that be to the LEA, to parents or possibly even an appeals tribunal or the Secretary of State for Education.

SIGNIFICANT LEARNING DIFFICULTIES AND ASSESSMENT-THROUGH-TEACHING

Children invariably come to the attention of their teachers as possibly

Table 6.6
Reasons for Keeping Curriculum-Based Records

Assessment Purpose	Assessment Emphasis
Record what child has already learned	Retrospective and Cumulative summary
Record how child has been taught in the past	Retrospective
Help to decide where to start teaching	Curriculum placement
Help decide what to teach next	Prospective
Monitor child's response to teaching / Record current teaching approach	Effectiveness of current teaching
Ascertain child's rate of progress	Is the child meeting expectations?
Evaluate effectiveness of own teaching	Accountability
Information to pass on to teaching colleagues	Continuity of teaching
Information to make available to parents and advisory personnel	Co-operation and consultation

having a difficulty in learning because their attainment levels are some way behind those of their peers. They may also be seen as failing to make satisfactory progress and the concern expressed is that the current provision may not be sufficient to meet the child's educational needs.

The fact that a child is 'adrift' from his peers in learning skills in important areas of the curriculum cannot *necessarily* be taken to imply that the child has a learning difficulty. While it is a natural inference to make it is predicated by a number of assumptions, which may well not be borne out in reality.

A major assumption would be that the learning opportunities of children in such a position have been the same as, or equivalent to, that of their peers. This may well not be the case for three main reasons. First of all the child's attendance at school may have been irregular. Key stages in learning various skills could have been missed through either absence or a change of school. It is not unusual for children transferring from one school to another to experience a number of problems arising directly from having to adjust to a completely new social environment. Often records accompanying the child arrive late or are an incomplete guide to current attainment levels and educational needs.

This and other circumstances give rise to the second reason for a child's learning opportunities being different from those of peers; the teaching offered may be inappropriate to meet the child's needs and so be ineffective in promoting learning. A child being exposed to teaching which is *not geared to his individual needs* cannot reasonably be seen as failing to learn or experiencing a learning difficulty.

The third reason emerges from the distinction drawn between *scheduled* and *engaged* teaching time. The former refers to the amount of time allocated during the school day when a child is time-tabled to take part in certain activities, for example a series of reading activities to be followed by a series of arithmetic exercises. Scheduling time for learning different skills cannot automatically be equated with the child being actively *engaged* in learning on the allotted activities. What may happen is the child spends time chatting to friends, or moves round the classroom to collect materials or sharpen a pencil, all of which *may* be valid in their own right but inevitably detracting from the time set aside to be working on the specified task. It cannot therefore be automatically assumed that scheduled teaching time becomes engaged teaching time. A growing body of research has been carried out on the effects of what is called 'academic engaged time' (e.g. Rosenshine and Berliner, 1978), and it is clearly a crucial factor in children's learning.

These factors should be remembered when considering whether or not a child has a learning difficulty. It is quite possible that the problems experienced by a pupil arise from a lack of *learning opportunities* rather than being the result of a difficulty in learning. It is only the period of continuous assessment which will demonstrate why a child's level of attainments are not commensurate with those of his peers.

A number of stages are involved in attempting to ascertain whether a child has a 'significantly greater difficulty in learning than the majority of children of his age'. Unfortunately the process is not as clear cut as implied in the definition of a learning difficulty. As was mentioned in Chapter 3, to refer to a child's difficulty in learning as being significantly greater than the majority of children of his age, creates the impression that such a decision can be made with a statistical precision and exactitude that is not possible in reality.

A starting point would be to identify the relevant peer group with which comparisons are to be made. The most valid comparisons would naturally seem to be with children from the same catchment area attending the same school. This is the only peer group that a teacher has direct access to, in order to make judgements about the attainment levels of the child considered to be experiencing difficulties and other pupils of a similar age and social background. The more removed the comparison group, the less reliable and therefore valid any subsequent conclusions would be.

The child who is thought to have a learning difficulty will be failing to meet teacher expectations in some way. This might arise through the pupil's attainment levels being behind those of peers or his rate of progress not being as rapid as peers.

In either case it is implied that the teacher knows both the attainment levels and rates of progress of peers. Equally, even if peers are not the yardstick against which comparisons are made, the implication is that the teacher is employing criteria by which a child's progress can be evaluated and that expectations, irrespective of how they are derived, are not being met. Within this population there are potentially two groups of children: those who, after subsequent investigation, prove to have a learning difficulty and those who do not and respond favourably to the teaching they receive.

To proceed with an assessment-through-teaching approach, harbouring the view that the child being assessed actually has a difficulty in learning *pre-empts* the whole process. Assessment-through-teaching, as well as identifying children's needs and provision to meet those needs, is also providing the framework through which a decision can be taken about whether or not a child has a learning difficulty. The only way of finding out whether a child actually does have a difficulty in learning is to teach him systematically, over a period of time, and carefully monitor and evaluate the pupil's learning outcomes.

For practical purposes therefore, it is important to see the period of assessment as contributing to an understanding of whether a child has a difficulty in learning, rather than to assume that this has already been established by virtue of initiating an assessment in the first place.

The process of assessment-through-teaching looks at how a child is taught and relates this to any learning that takes place. The first questions to be asked are, Is the child responding to teaching, is he learning? What teaching arrangements are facilitating these improvements? What form does the teaching take? What materials are being used, how much time is involved, how much practice is required? This information also needs to be looked at in the light of the effects it has on other members of the class. Are they still continuing to improve and make progress?

As well as knowing whether the child is learning, it is important to look at this progress in relation to his peers and ask the question, 'Is the child learning in such a way that he is beginning to catch up with his peers?'

These are the basic questions which precede any decisions about whether the child has a learning difficulty or the type of provision that is going to be most suitable. The following scenarios could be the result of the assessment period:

— the child is not responding to teaching and is not learning,
— the child is responding to teaching and is learning, but only slowly. As far as it is possible to make predictions on the basis of the data collected so far, the child is not catching up with his peers,

— the child is responding to teaching, is learning and is beginning to catch up with his peers. However, the gap is large and it may be some time before the child is performing at a level commensurate with his peers,

— the child is responding to teaching, is learning and is beginning to catch up with his peers. If progress continues to be maintained at this level the child might be performing at a level commensurate with his peers by (approximate date).

It is relatively easy to identify children at either end of this continuum, those children who are making almost no progress in response to systematic, carefully monitored and evaluated teaching; or those who make tremendous progress and come on in leaps and bounds. Most teachers will have had the satisfaction of teaching a child who at the beginning of the school year was a long way behind, but over the ensuing months made rapid progress and actually caught up his peers or was well on the road to doing so. In most respects they are not the ones that create the problems of decision-making. It is when children fall somewhere between the extremes of the continuum that the decisions are usually less clear-cut.

It is not possible and is potentially misleading to think that deciding a child has a 'significantly greater difficulty in learning than the majority of children of his age' can be achieved in a purely 'scientific' way. As so many of us surround ourselves with the new technology of the 1980s, microwave ovens, dishwashers, compact discs, it is tempting to imagine that scientists have also evolved a means of reliably and validly measuring a child's 'difficulty in learning'.

At present, the basis for making this decision as a teacher is the data collected during the assessment period, consultation with parents and other professionals and finally (though not least) professional judgement. The decision will ultimately depend on a variety of factors which relate specifically to an individual child and his particular school environment. To try and advance an all-embracing formula to answer the dilemma would be to ignore specific circumstances and the inevitable avalanche of exceptions to any proposed general rule!

However, there are a number of useful questions which should be addressed and discussed during consultations with parents, colleagues and other professionals. We summarise these in Table 6.7.

Probably the most useful criterion to apply when answering the questions and establishing whether the child has a learning difficulty and, considering the educational implications of this, is the notion of *'reasonableness'*. Given the information to hand, collected over a period of time in the prevailing conditions at school, what is the reasonable conclusion to draw about the child? Can the decision reached be supported by the data collected? This should be the main concern, making a reasonable series of decisions based on the available evidence.

Table 6.7
Some Useful Questions in Ascertaining the Extent of a Child's Learning Difficulty

---

How *long* has the child attended the present school?
How *regularly* has the child attended?
Has the child missed any *critical* periods of his education in the past?
What are the child's *current attainment levels* in relation to expectations:
  (a) prior to the assessment?
  (b) following the assessment?
What is the child's *rate of progress* in relation to expectations?
How long was the assessment-through-teaching period?
How does the child *respond* to teaching?
Is the child *learning*?
Is the child *catching up* with his peers?
What teaching *arrangements* have been made?
What provision is necessary to meet the child's needs?
If the child is making progress, and given existing provision, what is the likelihood of the child catching up with his peers and when would you anticipate this might happen?

At the outset of this discussion, we emphasised that within the group of children who may be thought to have a difficulty in learning, there will be those for whom the hypothesis is substantiated during the assessment period. For others, the hypothesis may not be so substantiated. This creates an interesting problem.

Let us concentrate first of all on the child who has a learning difficulty. Having a 'significantly greater difficulty in learning' must be taken to mean that the child's needs cannot be met with existing provision and that special educational provision is called for. 'A child has "special educational needs" if he has a learning difficulty which calls for special educational provision to be made for him' (Section 1 (1) Education Act 1981).

The highly idiosyncratic nature of the decision arises through its direct links with what is already being provided. This particular issue was discussed in Chapter 3. To reiterate, whether a child has a special educational need is determined not only by the nature of the learning difficulty but also by whether additional provision is necessary in accordance with Section 3 of the 1981 Education Act. If therefore a child has a learning difficulty and requires additional provision (i.e. special educational provision), he has a special educational need. However, if on the other hand he had a learning difficulty, but his needs are being met with existing provision, the child does not have a 'special educational need' as special educational provision is not required.

This in effect means that whether a child has a 'significantly greater difficulty in learning than the majority of children of his age' is determined by whether special educational provision is necessary. If it is, the learning difficulty is 'significantly greater, etc.' and if it is not, the learning difficulty is not significantly greater.

However it is also possible that an occasion will arise where a child (perhaps a third or fourth year junior or possibly of secondary school age):
— is a long way behind his peers,
— is making excellent progress,
— does not therefore have a difficulty in learning (by our criteria),
— but requires additional provision (special educational provision) to meet his needs so he can bridge the attainment gap with his peers. It is considered that without the additional provision the gap will not be bridged because the pupil is such a long way behind his peers.

The Act assumes that all children who are assessed under Section 5 have a difficulty in learning. What needs to be determined within its terms of reference is whether they have special educational needs as a result of requiring special educational provision. We have suggested that there are a number of dangers in adopting this position. Nevertheless, once the distinction has been made and the warnings heeded, when it comes to recommending that special educational provision is required, it may be necessary to take a purely pragmatic stance, and state the child has a learning difficulty to secure the appropriate provision, even though the data shows the child can make rapid progress. His current position and status in relation to peers would be attributable to lack of learning opportunities rather than a difficulty in learning.

SUMMARY

This chapter and Chapter 5 have described two approaches to assessment which we have characterised through the analogy of taking a 'snapshot' or 'video'. The 'snapshot' refers to the ways in which a static picture may not always tell the whole story. Sometimes all we may be able to achieve is a 'snapshot'. When this is the case it would be appropriate to indicate that the resulting picture of the child's needs may not be as comprehensive as would have been possible with a 'video'. Every effort must then be made to ensure that the 'snapshot' is in sharp focus. The 'video' on the other hand is concerned with a *continuous* appraisal of how a child is learning in the light of interventions undertaken in the classroom. It provides greater detail about how best to teach through offering feedback on a child's responses to different learning environments over a period of time.

FURTHER READING

Ainscow, M. and Tweddle, D. (1979). *Preventing Classroom Failure: An Objectives Approach*, John Wiley, London.

An easy-to-read, practical account of how the principles of assessment-through-teaching can be applied to teaching children with special needs.

Blankenship, C. and Lilly, S. (1981). *Mainstreaming Pupils with Learning and Behaviour Problems*, Holt, Rinehart and Winston, New York.
An excellent account of planning how to teach children with learning and behaviour difficulties within the framework of continuous assessment.

Gulliford, R. (1983). The school's role in assessment. *Special Education/ Forward Trends* **10**, 4, 6–9.
Discusses the importance of school-based assessment and the resources available to help teachers, in the context of the Warnock Report and 1981 Education Act.

Howell, K., Kaplan, J. and O'Connell, C. (1979). *Evaluating Exceptional Children : a Task Analysis Approach*, Chas. E. Merrill, Columbus, Ohio.
A good American source book on curriculum-based and criterion-referenced assessment and formative evaluation.

Smith, C. (ed.) (1985). *New Directions in Remedial Education*, The Falmer Press, London.
A useful collection of chapters introducing some recent trends in teaching and assessing children with learning difficulties.

Solity, J. E. and Bull, S. J. (1987). *Special Needs : Bridging the Curriculum Gap*, Open University Press, Milton Keynes.
Describes Task Analysis, Direct Instruction and Precision Teaching in relation to children with special needs. It demonstrates their complementary nature, shows how they can be applied in the classroom within the broad framework of assessment-through-teaching.

Solity, J.E. (1988). Systematic Assessment and Teaching–In Context. *In* G. Thomas and A. Feiler (eds) *Planning for Special Needs*, pp. 186-208, Blackwell, Oxford.
A description of specific teaching methods for teaching children who may have learning difficulties in the ordinary school. These methods are related to Haring and Eaton's instructional hierarchy.

Chapter Seven

THE STATUTORY ASSESSMENT PROCEDURE

In the preceeding three chapters we have offered an interpretation of the Education Act 1981, based on what we perceive to be the principles inherent in Circular 1/83. The discussion has centred around identifying the needs and making provision for the larger population of children who may experience difficulties in school, i.e. Warnock's 20%.

This chapter is concerned with the much smaller group of children who will become subjects of the statutory assessment procedure, initiated under Section 5 of the Act. We describe the role of the school in this procedure (within the framework of assessment-through-teaching) and place it in the context of the involvement and contributions of other professionals, parents and the LEA.

WHAT IS THE STATUTORY ASSESSMENT PROCEDURE?

This is the process of identifying a child's educational needs and the most appropriate provision to meet those needs under Sections 5 and 7 of the Education Act. It is sometimes referred to as *formal* assessment to distinguish it from other occasions when children are 'assessed'. The statutory assessment procedure relates to the process whereby three main professional groups: teachers, school medical officers and educational psychologists, are required to submit reports to the Director of Education, describing in their view, the educational needs of the child and the most suitable provision to meet the child's needs. The report each professional submits is referred to as 'advice' and how it *might* be prepared is explained separately in Chapter 8. It is within the advice that a school expresses its understanding and appreciation of a child's educational needs.

What might be a little confusing at this stage is the meaning of the term 'assessment'. It is a word, which depending on its context, will mean different things. In this chapter we are describing the *statutory assessment procedure*, which eventually refers to the administrative procedures undertaken in accordance with the 1981 Act and is interdisciplinary in nature.

In Chapter 6, we discussed an approach to *continuous assessment* known as *assessment-through-teaching*. This procedure was presented to help identify the needs of the broader school population and considers how this may be done over time, through monitoring and evaluating children's learning outcomes in response to the teaching they receive. Assessment-through-teaching is, in our view, a principle which should be incorporated into the statutory assessment procedure. Teachers may best fulfil their role within the statutory procedure by preparing their advice, on the basis of their understanding of the child derived from the assessment-through-teaching process.

As a result, once a child has become the subject of the statutory assessment procedure, much of what a teacher does on a daily basis need not change. The process of assessment-through-teaching is an integral part of effective classroom practice and should therefore be seen as an ongoing part of a child's education. However, there is considerable administrative activity outside the school, involving LEA officers, parents and other professionals. It is to these areas that this chapter is addressed.

There is, however, a new requirement on schools which would not necessarily have been part of 'everyday practice' which is the written advice submitted to the Director of Education. Although the information on which it is based may well already be available, schools do not usually prepare such a detailed written analysis of how a child has been taught.

It must also be remembered that ultimately, copies of the advice prepared by schools, educational psychologists and school medical officers are all sent to the parents to read. Similarly, the advice will invariably be seen by a range of personnel within the authority, for example advisors and administrators, and possibly by those external to the LEA in the event of parents contesting and appealing against the authority's decision. In some cases this could involve the Secretary of State for Education.

This aspect of the Act needs emphasising, not to increase the anxieties of the teacher, but to illustrate the very different nature and demands of advice writing, that hitherto have not been an aspect of the teacher's professional role. It does however, create the opportunity for those preparing advice, to demonstrate the range of expertise and quality of teaching that has taken place in relation to individual pupils over whom concern has been expressed. So, how does the process of seeking advice start?

MAKING A REQUEST FOR A STATUTORY ASSESSMENT

It is the Director of Education within an LEA who is notified about the possibility of the need to initiate the Statutory Assessment Procedure. He will be acting in response to concerns expressed, from a number of possible sources, about the probable educational needs of an individual pupil.

It is most likely to be a child's parent(s), guardian, or headteacher who first writes and draws the Director of Education's attention to the possibility that a child's needs are not being met in his existing school environment. However, on some occasions the initial request for a Statutory Assessment may come from another source, for example a school medical officer, psychologist, psychiatrist, paediatrician or social worker. Irrespective of its origins, the request has to be made in writing and present information to support the concerns being articulated. Most LEAs have issued guidelines on how this is to be done.

Schools can therefore instigate a statutory assessment and have the independent right to express their concerns about whether a child's educational needs are being met. However, it is to be hoped that before such a position is reached, prior consultations and negotiations would have been taking place with the various relevant support services, especially the Schools Psychological Services, as they are the only other LEA agency with an obligation to submit advice.

Of even greater importance is the contact and relationship established with parents. Parents are increasingly being involved in the education of their children, in many different capacities, and their early involvement when difficulties are being experienced is encouraged in the legislation. But it is also good practice to collaborate with parents in trying to overcome a child's difficulties. So where the school makes the initial request for an assessment, it would be reasonable to expect that the child's parents would already have been involved in a continuing dialogue, and discussions taken place with an educational psychologist or other services as appropriate.

INITIATING THE PROCEDURE

The Director of Education, after receiving the initial request from a school, the child's parents or any other professional person with a legitimate concern, has in the first place to decide whether:

> **there are prima facie grounds to suggest that a child's needs are such as to require provision additional to, or otherwise different from, the facilities and resources generally available in ordinary schools in the area under normal arrangements**
> **Circular 1/83, Paragraph 13**

It is expected that the deciding factors in determining prima facie grounds will vary from authority to authority depending on existing provision. If he is satisfied that prima facie grounds exist, an officer of the authority would write to parents in order to inform them:

> — that they propose to make an assessment;
> — of the procedure to be followed in making it;
> — of the name of the officer of the authority from whom further information could be obtained;

— of the right to make representations, and submit written evidence, to the authority within a period of not less than 29 days from the date on which the notice was served.

Education Act 1981, Section 5(3)

Such a procedure highlights the need for having previously consulted with parents. It is not difficult to imagine their reaction on receiving such information from the Director of Education without any prior consultation.

Should the request for an assessment come from the parents:

the authority shall comply with the request unless it is in their opinion unreasonable,

1981 Education Act, Section 9

No guidance is given in the Circular as to what might constitute an 'unreasonable' request, and no information is readily available to indicate how often parental requests are viewed as unreasonable or what the grounds are for such a decision.

STARTING THE ASSESSMENT PROCEDURE

Once a parent has been informed, and had the opportunity to respond to the LEA's intention to undertake a statutory assessment by the Director of Education, the school, educational psychologists and medical officers can be involved in the process. Their overall involvement is defined and described in the Education (Special Educational Needs) Regulations 1983.

In addition to the three profesional groups mentioned, advice might also be sought from any other source that the Director of Education might consider to be beneficial to the overall understanding of the child's educational needs.

WHO PROVIDES THE ADVICE?

Educational

Initially it is the headteacher of a school who receives the request for advice. It will then depend very much on school policy as to who actually writes the advice which is ultimately submitted to the LEA. The child should however, have been attending the school 'at some time within the preceding 18 months' (Regulations, Paragraph 5, (1) (a)). Where this is not the case for some reason, (perhaps the child has only recently entered the LEA), the authority needs to be satisified that the individual writing the advice 'has experience of teaching children with special educational needs or knowledge of the differing provision which may be called for in different cases to meet those needs' (Regulations, Paragraph (5) (1) (b)).

Where the headteacher has not had regular teaching contact with the pupil who is the subject of the advice, it is expected that consultations will take place with those teachers who have been responsible for carrying out the assessment and who are most likely to have a full understanding of the child's educational needs. Whoever prepares the written advice therefore, whether the headteacher or other designated member of staff, it is vital that the knowledge and views of those with the most frequent and relevant contact with the pupil are fully and accurately represented.

Medical

The medical advice will typically be written by 'a fully registered medical practitioner' who has been designated by the district health authority (usually a school medical officer) or is nominated by them (possibly a paediatrician and psychiatrist). Only a fully qualified doctor is able to offer advice on *medical* factors which may affect a child's educational needs.

Psychological

The psychological advice is provided by a member of the local authority schools psychological service and so will be an educational psychologist. Should another psychologist either from within the same LEA or a different LEA, or a clinical psychologist, have relevant information relating to ascertaining a child's educational needs, it is expected that their views should be sought and considered in the preparation of the advice.

Other Sources

There may be occasions when an authority feels that it would be of benefit to request advice from an additional source to those already mentioned, such as an advisory teacher for the hearing or visually impaired children.

The advice from the three principal contributors is accorded equal status, thus removing the tendency, prior to the introduction of the Act, whereby the educational psychologist's report was viewed as having greater weight than that of teachers. Swann (1982), for example, argued that educational psychologists acted as the 'gate keepers' to special schools. The new legislation should mean that no single professional group within the LEA, submitting advice, could be regarded as having greater influence over determining the outcomes of the process, than any other.

ISSUES TO CONSIDER DURING THE ASSESSMENT PROCEDURE

The Education (Special Educational Needs) Regulations (1983, Paragraph 8) remind all those preparing advice to be aware of, and acknowledge, the views of parents before submitting their written reports (see also Circular 1/83, Paragraph 43). The LEA will in fact provide the writers of advice with copies of any representations made by parents and any evidence submitted by, or at their request. This again emphasises the role which parents are able to take within the formal procedures and also underlines the importance of close collaboration with them, ideally throughout children's school careers, but especially during the statutory assessment procedure.

CO-OPERATION BETWEEN PROFESSIONALS

In keeping with the general principle of effective inter-disciplinary co-operation, the Education Act and Circular 1/83 urge those preparing advice to liaise with each other whenever this is appropriate. On some occasions, the LEA may well specify individuals who ought to be consulted because of the information and knowledge they are seen to have (Circular 1/83, Paragraph 22).

Circular 1/83 gives guidelines on the responsibilities of each professional following a dialogue with colleagues. They are reminded that the advice submitted is their own personal and professional responsibility (Paragraph 22). This should be viewed positively, particularly by teachers, as it acknowledges the contribution they have to make, reiterates their status and parity with school medical officers and educational psychologists and further emphasises their contribution within the context of being a 'professional adviser'. At a time when the role of teachers is coming under close scrutiny, it is perhaps heartening to see the professional stature of their work being recognised through legislation and being accorded equal standing to that of other professional groups.

Whilst close co-operation, collaboration and mutual support are warmly encouraged (Paragraph 34), each professional is required to respect the differing contributions of others and focus in advice writing, on the issues of *special relevance to themselves* (Paragraph 34). So, professional independence and responsibility is expected but not at the expense of inter-disciplinary co-operation.

PROFESSIONAL ASSESSMENT

In this section we are referring to the time required by each professional to assess a child's educational needs and the most suitable provision to meet those needs. This is the period when the child is the focus of attention and does not include the administrative functions fulfilled by an LEA of notifying parents, awaiting their responses, etc. In this sense, we are referring to the professional assessment which is undertaken within the context of the whole statutory assessment *procedure*.

No definitive information is available on the expected time scale, although this may change in future legislation, but clearly the numerous references to assessment being a 'continuous process' implies that it is not something that can be completed quickly, especially as teachers are expected to monitor the effects of different approaches to teaching on children's learning (Circular 1/83, Paragraph 11).

The main recommendation that can be offered in respect to this area of discussion is very much an obvious, common sense one, operating on the principle of what seems to be reasonable under a given set of circumstances. The time scale is likely to vary in relation to different children and the nature of their needs. What seems preferable is that advice should not be submitted before the professionals concerned feel they have sufficient information to give them a comprehensive understanding of the child's educational needs. However, it is appreciated that this will not aways be possible.

Should local circumstances dictate that advice is required before professionals feel they are in this position, they have at least two possible options. They could notify the LEA of the current position and state why they would appreciate more time to complete their assessment. If this is not acceptable, the advice subsequently prepared would necessarily have to reflect the professional's appraisal of the child's needs on the basis of the information currently available.

We have already talked about the type of continuous assessment which we would see as being of greatest value to teachers in determining children's educational needs (Chapter 6). Much the same could also be said of the assessment undertaken by educational psychologists. Ideally the records and data that would serve teachers most effectively would be the same for educational psychologists. This has obvious implications for the pattern of collaborations established between teachers and psychologists.

Teachers and educational psychologists have different but complementary areas of expertise. When applied jointly to the assessment process, these skills can lead to a much fuller appreciation of the child's needs and the most suitable provision to meet them, than if applied totally independently of each other. It is therefore desirable that teachers and psychologists consult at the earliest possible opportunity to plan the assessment process, and certainly earlier than is implied in Warnock's five stages of assessment.

However, although there are many persuasive arguments in favour of joint working in this way, the phrasing of the Education Act means that a psychologist may opt for a psychometrically orientated approach to assessment rather than one that is essentially curriculum based. As Cox (1985) points out, psychologists are at liberty to select either approach as neither is precluded in the legislation. The very nature of a traditionally psychometric assessment would have inevitable consequences for the collaboration between psychologists and teachers.

It is also worth noting that there are some, 'instances where a reliance upon psychological assessment might be regarded by the courts as "unreasonable".' For example: 'where the sole basis of assessment is a psychometric test administered to a child at a time of emotional trauma' (Cox, 1985, p. 44).

Where the assessment is psychometrically based, it will invariably take place outside the child's classroom, either elsewhere in the school or possibly an alternative venue, such as a Child Guidance Centre. On such occasions parents would be notified of their right to attend such an assessment.

In the event of both teacher and psychologist adopting a curriculum based approach to assessment, the notion of a 'single assessment' or 'examination' of the child is abandoned and so parents' rights with respect to their attendance at such occasions would have to be negotiated on a different basis, as is considered in Chapter 9.

On the other hand school medical officers have, in the majority of cases, far less contact with teachers than educational psychologists. Since their expertise is medical rather than educational, their assessment will probably take place at a separate venue to the school and be conducted on a single occasion. As a result, teachers are less likely to be involved in a continuing dialogue with members of the medical profession than they are with psychologists. As far as the content of the medical advice is concerned, Circular 1/83 (Paragraph 34) states that, 'doctors will draw attention to the implications of the child's medical condition, and to the support and facilities the child may require'.

COLLATING PROFESSIONAL REPORTS

Information by each professional is contained in a report known as *the advice*. Each professional group is given the same general information about the content of advice which is contained in the Regulations (Paragraph 4). From their own particular perspective, they are required to identify and comment on factors which are relevant to the child's educational needs. Furthermore, their views are sought on the provision to meet those needs whether that provision be rendered special or non-educational.

Inevitably LEAs vary considerably in the educational provision they have available at any time. Equally inevitable is the fact that on some occasions it will be felt that a child's needs can be best met by a particular form of provision, but one which is not available within the LEA. It is stated in Circular 1/83 (Paragraph 35) that advice should not be influenced by the eventual school placement since that is a matter to be determined by the LEA at a later stage. So although *specific* school placements cannot be mentioned in the advice, appropriate provision should be, but not in a way which might be seen as committing an LEA to a particular form of provision or placement, and thus pre-empting its decision.

Each professional is responsible for his or her own advice and so must feel confident that the opinions offered can be substantiated and give an accurate account of their understanding of the child's needs. No details are available on how the advice ought to be presented and so it is left to each professional to compile the advice in the way he or she considers most suitable.

Similarly, no single LEA officer is specifically designated as being the most appropriate individual to collate the advice. Although the advice is requested in the name of the Director of Education, it is extremely unlikely that the chief officer would assume this role in practice. In reality, it is likely to be an administrator, perhaps an Assistant Education Officer (AEO) for special education, an advisor for special education or an educational psychologist. In the case of it being an educational psychologist a dilemma could arise from having to wear two separate hats: one as an officer of the LEA trying impartially to assess the advice received from different professionals, the other as an independent professional submitting his own advice on the child's needs.

Some authorities have created a 'new breed' of administrator, namely the 'Statement Officer' or some similar title. The prime role would be seen as collating advice and preparing a draft statement based on the recommendations received. This might sometimes be done in consultation with other LEA administrators.

Again, flexibility is allowed in determining the order in which advice is submitted as it is recognised that this will, in part, be determined by local circumstances (Circular 1/83, Paragraph 32). The sequence mentioned in the Circular is educational, medical and finally psychological but this perhaps reflects a more traditional view of assessment or one which adheres to Warnock's five stages. In any event, it is recommended that copies of all the advice received should be sent to all the professionals advising on the child's needs.

What Happens Next?

Once all the advice has been received, it is then up to a designated LEA officer, acting on behalf of the Director of Education, to determine whether special educational provision is necessary to meet the child's educational needs. It should be pointed out that Circular 1/83 (Paragraph 39) makes it clear that:

> **the ultimate responsibility for assessing the child's special educational needs rests with the LEA.**

The various professionals offer their own views on the child's needs based on their assessments, but they only advise, rather than make a decision.

It is therefore in the nature of 'advice', that the LEA can accept or reject the advice they are given. Sometimes though the LEA may receive conflicting or incomplete advice, in which case before any decision can be reached, further discussions may be necessary. The LEA would therefore probably arrange a meeting of those having submitted advice to try and resolve existing conflicts. If this is not possible the responsibility then rests with the LEA to decide on the weighting to be accorded each piece of advice.

This further emphasises the importance of being able to substantiate views presented with appropriate data collected over a period of time. It would seem inevitable that, in general, less credence will be attached to an opinion based on information collected on a single occasion rather than that collected systematically and continuously over a period of time, or at least on a number of occasions.

Ultimately a decision has to be made and the LEA will decide that the child either has or has not got special educational needs. When it is felt the child has special educational needs a statement will be prepared.

PREPARING STATEMENTS ON CHILDREN'S SPECIAL EDUCATIONAL NEEDS

Figure 7.1 contains a copy of the recommended format for a Statement of Special Educational Needs, in five parts. The appendices listed A to G, which are attached to the Statement are presented in Figure 7.2.

The Statement is at first provisional and is sent, together with the appendices, to the child's parents (or guardians). They then have 15

Part I	— Introduction, setting out basic details about the child.
Part II	— A decision of the child's special educational needs.
Part II	— The provision to meet the needs described in Part II, which may be in terms of facilities and equipment, staffing arrangments or otherwise (Regulations, Paragraph 10 (1) a).
Part IV	— The school, type of school or possibly education provided elsewhere, other than at a school.
Part V	— Non-educational provision such as may be offered by a district health authority, social services department or some other body.

Figure 7.1 Format for a Statement of Special Educational Needs.

Appendix A	Parental representations — this would include written representations and a summary, accepted by the parent as accurate of any oral representations made.
Appendix B	Parental evidence — submitted by the parent or at the request of a parent.
Appendix C	Educational advice.
Appendix D	Medical advice
Appendix E	Psychological advice.
Appendix F	Other advice obtained by the LEA.
Appendix G	Information furnished by District Health Authority or Social Services Authority.

Figure 7.2   Appendices to the Statement.

days in which to respond, either agreeing with its contents or requesting further discussions with representatives of the LEA. If they agree with the provisions of the Statement, the proposed version then becomes the substantive one.

As far as the school is concerned, there are two possible consequences of the statementing procedure, both of which have resource implications. It must be remembered that a child will only be deemed to have special educational needs when some form of special educational provision is required to meet those needs. The provision made available will be additional to that already available and could take the form of additional resources being placed in the child's existing, mainstream school. Alternatively the child's needs might be met by a placement in another school offering different educational provision. It is likely that before parents accept the latter form of provision they would be invited to visit any potential new school for their child. This was standard practice prior to the 1981 Education Act and is recommended in the new legislation (Circular 1/83, Paragraph 49). A school should expect to know which of these alternatives is being offered by an LEA and considered by parents, before the proposed Statement becomes substantive.

DECIDING NOT TO PROVIDE A STATEMENT

After considering the presented advice, the LEA may decide that the child does not require special educational provision and therefore is not deemed as having special educational needs. The implication here would be that existing resources are suitable and capable of meeting the child's educational needs.

The speed with which a school can expect to hear from the LEA on the intended course of action, following the completion and submission of advice will vary from authority to authority. It would depend on the number of cases currently going through the procedure, the availability of educational psychologists and medical officers to complete the respective psychological and medical advices and the demands being made on the LEA officer designated as being responsible for co-ordinating the procedure.

What is known, and has already been stated, is that parents have up to 15 days to respond on hearing the LEA decision. If this is accepted, a school could expect to be notified of this reasonably quickly. If the parents do not agree with the LEA's formulation, they may appeal, and depending on the nature and circumstances surrounding the appeal, a final decision may be some time in the making.

APPEALS

A parent may appeal against the content of a Statement once it has been issued in its substantive form. The specific details of the procedure are contained in Section 8 of the 1981 Education Act. In essence the appeal would initially be to an appeal committee who would confirm the provision in the Statement or ask the LEA to reconsider their decision. After being informed of the committee's deliberations the parents may then, if still not satisfied, appeal in writing to the Secretary of State. The Secretary of State after consulting with the LEA could then:
— confirm the provision specified in the Statement,
— amend the Statement,
— direct the LEA to cease to maintain the Statement.

Clearly all of this would take a considerable amount of time and no indication is given in the legislation as to what the maximum time scale for such a series of negotiations could reasonably be expected to be. In the meantime, the likelihood is that the child concerned would remain in his current school until a final decision is made.

A parent can also appeal directly in writing to the Secretary of State if an LEA decides that it would not be in order to prepare a Statement, since in their view, the child does not require special educational provision and cannot therefore be said to have special educational needs. However, under these circumstances the most the Secretary of State can do is ask the LEA to reconsider their decision. He is not empowered to direct them to change their decision as he is once a Statement has actually been issued.

A time delay here would presumably not be as serious as one occurring due to an appeal against a Statement, principally because in the view of the LEA the child's educational needs were being met with the provision available in the child's current school.

It is interesting to note that there is no provision in the legislation for those submitting advice to appeal against the LEA's decision. They cannot, for example, suggest that their advice has been ignored or misinterpreted. That is the sole perogative of the parents.

REVIEWS

Every Statement issued by the LEA has to be reviewed at least annually. According to Circular 1/83 (Paragraph 55) the basis of the review is a report prepared by the child's school. It should reflect the views of teachers, other professionals and those of parents. Significantly the annual review should be seen 'as part of a process of continuous assessment', a further endorsement that assessment should be an integral aspect of everyday teaching.

Where a child has had a Statement issued in relation to his special educational needs and is being taught in a mainstream school, the responsibility for completing the review would in the main rest with that school.

REASSESSMENTS

Reassessments can arise in two ways. First of all, it may be felt that there has been a significant change in the child's circumstances, with the result that current provision may well not be meeting the child's needs. A reassessment can, therefore, be requested by anyone with a legitimate concern, for example: parents, school, other professionals. In effect, this involves re-starting the formal assessment procedure in relation to a child who is already the subject of a Statement.

Alternatively, where a child's needs have not been assessed before he reached the age of 12 years 6 months, they must be reassessed in the year following the day on which the pupil reached the age of 13 years 6 months. The reassessment would also be the responsibility of the ordinary school if that was the child's current place of education. As this process happens automatically at a certain age for all children on whom a Statement is maintained, it is known as a *statutory reassessment*. The purpose of the statutory reassessment is:

> to enable attention to be given to the arrangements to be made for the child during the remainder of his time at school, to his preparation for the transition to adult life, and to the nature of the further education, vocational training, employment or other arrangements to be made for the child when he leaves school,
>
> Circular 1/83, Paragraph 56

SUMMARY

This chapter has looked at the details of the Statutory Assessment

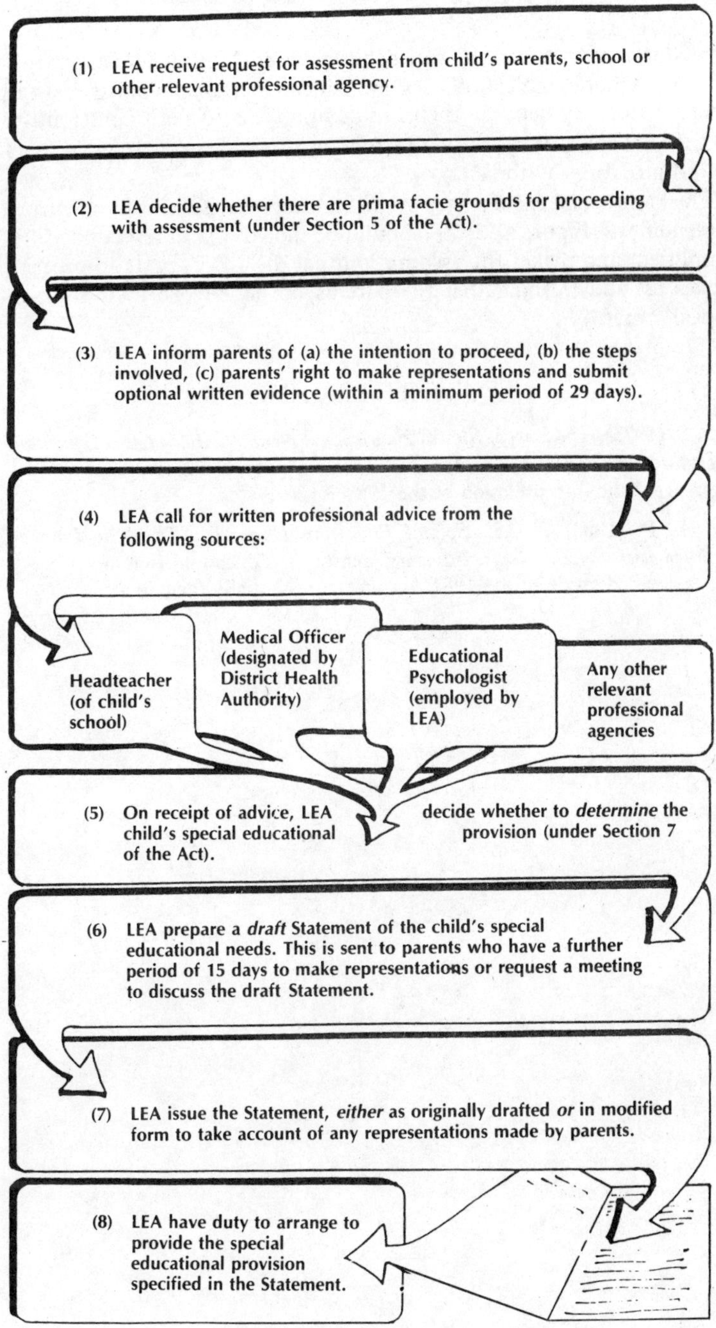

(1) LEA receive request for assessment from child's parents, school or other relevant professional agency.

(2) LEA decide whether there are prima facie grounds for proceeding with assessment (under Section 5 of the Act).

(3) LEA inform parents of (a) the intention to proceed, (b) the steps involved, (c) parents' right to make representations and submit optional written evidence (within a minimum period of 29 days).

(4) LEA call for written professional advice from the following sources:

Headteacher (of child's school)

Medical Officer (designated by District Health Authority)

Educational Psychologist (employed by LEA)

Any other relevant professional agencies

(5) On receipt of advice, LEA child's special educational decide whether to *determine* the provision (under Section 7 of the Act).

(6) LEA prepare a *draft* Statement of the child's special educational needs. This is sent to parents who have a further period of 15 days to make representations or request a meeting to discuss the draft Statement.

(7) LEA issue the Statement, *either* as originally drafted *or* in modified form to take account of any representations made by parents.

(8) LEA have duty to arrange to provide the special educational provision specified in the Statement.

Figure 7.3 The Statutory Assessment Procedure: Basic Sequence.

Procedure. It described the role of the three main professional groups: teachers, school medical officers and educational psychologists and the inter-relationship between them. In addition the teacher's contribution to the procedure was set in the context of the general requirements placed on LEAs by the Act.

The basic sequence of stages in the Statutory Assessment Procedure is presented in Figure 7.3. It should be noted that the sequence is simplified, and makes the assumption that the LEA decide to proceed (boxes (2) and (5)) and that the parents do not invoke their right to appeal (box (6)).

FURTHER READING

Cox, B. (1975). *The Law of Special Educational Needs: A Guide to the Education Act 1981*, Croom Helm, London.

A legalistic interpretation of the 1981 Act.

Newell, P. (1983). *A.C.E. Special Education Handbook: The New Law on Children with Special Needs*, Advisory Centre for Education, London.

A detailed guide to the 1981 Act written essentially for parents.

Chapter Eight

PREPARING REPORTS ON CHILDREN WITH SPECIAL EDUCATIONAL NEEDS

INTRODUCTION

The report submitted by the child's current school when his educational needs are being assessed under the 1981 Act, is known as 'the educational advice'. This report represents a new role for teachers since it is the first time they have been required to submit information on a child's needs to an LEA by an Act of Parliament. This clearly presents a challenge for teachers to demonstrate their expertise and ability to identify and describe the nature of a child's educational needs to parents, administrators and other professionals.

The task of writing advice may understandably be viewed with apprehension by many teachers, as it is an aspect of their role for which they may have received less than adequate preparation. Many will have trained before any such demands were being made on teachers through the new legislation. Recent entrants to the profession are unfortunately not likely to be better placed. Although all initial teacher training courses are now required to have a special needs component, it is unlikely that sufficient time will have been available to go into the necessary detail of compiling and writing advice. Other professionals on the other hand, are trained over a number of years in this area and spend most of their working lives dealing with children with special needs. So teachers, at least initially, are at some disadvantage with respect to preparing reports on children presenting difficulties.

You will be able to infer from what has been written so far in this book, that while many interpretations can be made about the 1981 Education Act, the one presented within these pages is a positive one. So it is also with respect to writing advice.

In Chapter 2, it was suggested that many of the details of the Education Act and its associated legislation, encapsulated many of the recent trends in special education and represented current thinking in the area of special needs. Writing advice could be seen as the 'tip of the iceberg' with respect to good practice. The advice can only ever be as good as the work on which it is based, which will have been taking place in the weeks, months or years prior to its completion.

The written advice should, in our view, be based largely on the regular records kept on children's progress and development. Circular

1/83 recognises this link when it states: 'Teachers should be encouraged to keep full records of their pupils' progress and to include information about professional consultations and assessments' (Paragraph 11). The value of keeping detailed records on children which can guide teachers in their daily interactions with pupils in the classroom, has been stressed outside the confines of special education. DES publications, textbooks for teachers, etc., all emphasise the importance of an effective record-keeping system for carefully monitoring and evaluating children's progress and for planning future work.

The need therefore for schools to develop their own record-keeping systems is well documented. The Education Act does not usher in a new age, giving increased prominence to keeping records at the expense of other facets of the teacher's role. Instead it is best viewed as acknowledging the relevance of such records to effective classroom practice. In so doing, the Act inevitably highlights general issues about the importance of keeping records on all children, not just those who might be thought of as having special educational needs.

There are two possible occasions on which advice will need to be prepared by schools. The first will be during the initial assessment of a child's educational needs, initiated under Section 5 of the 1981 Education Act. The second, is when parents ask for a reassessment of their child's special educational needs (Section 9 (2)) or when a child has reached the appropriate age for statutory reassessment, as described in the preceding chapter. In each of these instances, the formal assessment procedure is followed and advice is submitted to the LEA by educational psychologists and school medical officers in addition to teachers.

WHAT ARE SCHOOLS EXPECTED TO WRITE?

At this point, let us consider what schools, along with the other professional groups are *asked* to provide in their written advice (DES Circular 1/83, Paragraph 23).

Each professional adviser should aim to give the appropriate professional view of the child's needs in terms of:
(i) the relevant aspects of the child's functioning, including his strengths and weaknesses, his relation with his environment at home and at school, and any relevant aspects of the child's past history.
(ii) the aims to which provision for the child should be directed to enable him to develop educationally and increase his independence.
(iii) the facilities and resources recommended to promote the achievement of these aims.

Circular 1/83 goes on to acknowledge that the checklist offered in Annex 1 (presented in Appendix 1) is intented as an *aide-mémoire* only and may need to be varied according to the circumstances of particular cases. It is also expected that LEAs may choose to provide schools with structured forms of their own design.

In view of this, we do not intend to provide a definitive format for writing advice. Instead, we consider a number of guidelines and offer a framework within which this task can be completed. The focus of the chapter is therefore the information to be included in the advice, the type of records through which it can be documented and some general principles for assembling and formulating advice. Although we are writing specifically in relation to preparing reports on children with special needs, we hope the principles outlined will have a broader application beyond the specific requirements of the Act.

GOOD PRACTICE WHEN WRITING ADVICE

The advice once written and submitted to the LEA becomes a public document. Initially it will be read, and its contents considered, by the designated officer of the LEA, who will place its recommendations alongside those of the educational psychologist and school medical officer. It will subsequently be included in its entirety, in the documents sent to parents once the LEA has determined whether or not the child has special educational needs. In the event of parents appealing against the LEA's decision, the appeals committee would see the advice as might the Secretary of State for Education, should the parents fail to be satisfied with the LEA's response to their child's needs.

Each of these groups will come into the formal assessment process at a different stage, and with the obvious exception of the parents, will never have met the child and so will not know the pupil in question. It is important to remember, therefore, that the advice will probably be required to fulfil different functions, depending on who is reading it and for what purpose.

It should also be recognised that, whilst those reading the advice will have the brief of trying to gain an understanding of the child's needs and the provision best suited to meet those needs, it is inevitable that impressions will also be formed about those who have actually prepared the advice. Marshall McLuhan coined what is now a well known phrase, 'the medium is the message' (Postman and Weingartner, 1969). In other words, what is often more relevant than what we say is how we say it. The image of the second-hand car salesman epitomises this aphorism. We can hear and understand the words of the salesman's pitch, but somehow it just does not ring true. There is something about the way the message is delivered that invariably does not convince and so suggests caution on our part. How the advice is compiled, and the way it is articulated will inevitably reflect something about the person writing it, as it will about the child in question.

Those writing advice therefore have a responsibility to give a positive account of their own professional skills and those of colleagues, who may have worked with the child, as well as of the pupil. In a sense it is not just the child that is 'on show', but the school as well.

However, teachers start from a position of strength. They will usually be more familiar with the child (with the exception of the parents) than either of the other professional groups submitting advice, or those who have the responsibility of making decisions about the child's educational needs. They will also have been able to work with the child over a period of time, in a range of different settings, and so are well placed to undertake a thorough assessment of the child's strengths and weaknesses and reach an informed understanding of the child's educational needs.

The parents and child about whom a report is being prepared, have a right to expect that the information presented will adhere to certain principles, which will help ensure it is an accurate representation of existing circumstances. In our view, the questions presented in Table 8.1 should remain uppermost in the minds of those involved in writing advice.

Table 8.1
Questions to be Addressed in the Preparation of Advice

Is the professional information presented on the child and his needs *valid?*
Is the information *reliable?*
Is the information *fair?*
Is the information *comprehensive* in its coverage of the child's strengths and weaknesses?
Is the information presented in a way that can be readily *understood?*
Acid Test: Would you like *your* child to be written about in this way?

Is the Information Valid?

Schools will have to hand a mass of information on children, especially when they have been at the school over a number of years. The information included in the advice has to be relevant to the questions being raised. These essentially are: 'What are the child's present educational needs?' and 'What provision will best meet those needs?' The information therefore has to be pertinent to these questions, as well as trying to paint a general picture of the child and his overall level of functioning in the classroom and school environments. Those reading the advice will not be as familiar with the child as the teacher, and so will find it helpful to have a framework in which to place the analysis of the child's needs and the suggestions on the most suitable provision to meet the needs.

Is the Information Reliable?

Can the views contained in the advice be justified? Are they supported by relevant data? One way of estimating whether these criteria can be met is to imagine being questioned about the source of the details contained in the advice, by a Perry Mason like figure. Consider each opinion offered and ask yourself, 'How do you know this? On what data are your views based? When was the data collected? How up-to-date is it? Why do you think the stated provision is most suitable? Do you have any way of supporting this opinion?'

If the courtroom scenario sounds a little remote or fanciful, these may well be the questions of those reading the advice. It will have considerably greater credibility and weight if the views represented are supported by relevant data. In addition, it would be important to give details of who said what and to make it clear what the sources of information were.

Is the Information Fair?

One of the most important things to guard against when writing advice is allowing personal feelings and prejudices to influence its contents. It is inevitable that on some occasions, some children will evoke strong reactions in their teachers, which could possibly affect their perceptions of those individuals. This is more likely to occur when a child has had a disruptive effect in the classroom.

Presenting information that is both valid and reliable will go some way towards preventing the likelihood of this happening. However, it is worth restating that what is often as important as *what* is written, is *how* it is written. Personal bias could also be influenced in the language used in the advice and again every effort should be made to ensure that the information presented and written style is free from prejudice and bias and can thus be seen to be balanced and fair.

Is the Information Comprehensive?

Does the information offer a comprehensive account of how the child is performing in the classroom? Sometimes, when reporting on children experiencing difficulties there is a natural tendency to focus on what they *cannot* do or on the areas posing problems. Circular 1/83 draws attention to the need to look carefully at a child's strengths, his skills and personal attributes. We are reminded of the line from the popular song: 'You've got to accentuate the positive, Eliminate the negative; Latch on to the affirmative, Don't mess with Mr. In-Between'.

The advice has to try and paint a full picture of the child, so that those who are not familiar with him can obtain an accurate impression of what he is like in a range of different circumstances. The more careful and systematic the teacher's observations, and thorough the evaluation of progress over time, the more comprehensive will be the resulting details contained in the advice. The aim should be to passs on the things that have been *learned* about the most effective ways of working with a pupil and to support the views presented with suitable evidence.

Can the Information be Understood?

The advice will be read by a number of people with different levels of experience in the field of children with special needs. There is a fine balance to be achieved between presenting the information in a detailed and meaningful way, while at the same time ensuring its readability and accessibility.

Members of a profession often use words and expressions which have become second nature to them, without always appreciating the effects on those who may be hearing them for the first time. Many of us will at some time have been on the receiving end of 'jargon' from doctors, lawyers, accountants or other such professionals. This can be highly confusing and uncomfortable. No more desirable, however, is information which is over-simplified and potentially patronising.

The word 'jargon' is invariably viewed as having pejorative overtones, and to use 'jargon' is also seen in a less than positive light. Jargon is defined in the Concise Oxford Dictionary as 'a mode of speech familiar only to a group or profession'. There are clearly phrases and expressions associated with mainstream and special education that have little meaning to the woman or man in the street unfamiliar with these fields.

However, to write advice without using some specialised words may, in our view, be extremely difficult and could possibly render the information presented as over-simplified or being liable to misinterpretation. Furthermore, it may carry less weight when examined in detail, as might happen during an appeals procedure.

When writing advice, the teacher has to be sensitive to these issues and recognise who will be reading it, from what background and for what purposes. The parents will be least familiar with the language typically used in educational circles, and we discuss in detail in Chapter 9 what we consider to be the most suitable ways of working with parents in general and within the specific context of the Education Act 1981.

The advice must therefore be meaningful, make its points succinctly and present evidence that will substantiate the views forwarded. This will almost inevitably involve using some language and terminology in general usage within education but perhaps not outside, so every attempt should be made to ensure it is essential, kept to a minimum and explained where appropriate.

The Acid Test

The guideline that is most helpfully borne in mind when preparing advice is the one we have called *the acid test*. Place yourself in the position of the parent who is reading the advice which you have written. Ask whether you would be happy if your child had been written about *in this way*. Is an accurate and fair portrait conveyed that is valid, reliable and well-informed? Is the underlying tone one which suggests that the writer has gained insights into the child's needs and feels positively orientated towards him? There will certainly be occasions when parents and teachers may have to agree to *differ* in their interpretation of the child's needs. We believe however, that when the teacher's views are communicated sensitively as being in the best interests of the child, parents usually respect the teacher's professionalism and integrity.

It is also important that the advice is viewed from a professional standpoint. If the above criteria are met then it is likely that the teacher concerned would have presented the LEA, parents and others with a positive image of the school and colleagues who have worked with the child. It will be apparent that opinions ventured are supported by appropriate evidence and compiled systematically and comprehensively over a period of time.

GETTING INFORMATION READY

The process of collecting information, of course, starts well before the advice is written. The most valuable information to include is that which is collected over time and demonstrates the extent to which existing resources have been employed to try to meet a child's needs. This would be an example of preparing a 'video' of a child's recent school experiences rather than a series of 'snapshots'. As we suggested in Chapter 7 the snapshot omits many of the necessary contextual details required to convey a comprehensive account of the child's progress. The 'video' on the other hand conveys a much fuller picture of the child's response to prevailing circumstances.

The purpose of the advice is to inform the LEA of the school's views on the nature of a child's educational needs. These will emerge from the assessment-through-teaching process (see Chapter 6) and will be based on how the child has responded to the educational arrangements made for him.

Details of the Assessment-Through-Teaching for Children with Learning Difficulties

It is often difficult to distil all the information collected through a continuous assessment procedure, so that the salient points are made without omitting any important details. This is especially true when the advice potentially has such a wide and varied audience.

In essence, this part of the advice will talk the reader through the

school's efforts in recent weeks or months in ascertaining and trying to meet the child's needs. It will cover the child's learning experiences in each of the major basic skills curriculum areas (reading, numeracy, language, writing). This will incorporate descriptions of:
— the child's current attainment levels in each basic skill area, i.e. the skills the child has learned in each of these areas according to the curriculum being followed by the school;
— a comparison between the level of skills acquired by the child and those of his peers.

The above two pieces of information are collected in terms of time, as near as possible to when the advice is being written, the intention being to make sure the information provided is up to date. These details are necessarily *summative*, offering an overview, in the form of a 'snapshot' of what children have learned at a particular moment in time. The other information collected through assessment-through-teaching is *formative*, and includes details of a child's rate of progress over time throughout the period of continuous assessment. The information here would include:
— Details of the child's attainment levels in basic skill areas at the beginning of the assessment-through-teaching process.
— The teaching arrangements made for the child. These would include details of methods of teaching and relevant aspects of classroom organisation. As many details as possible are noted so that children's learning outcomes can be directly related to the specific conditions which helped promote them. This approach requires that changes to any aspect of the teaching environment, if and when they occur, are introduced systematically, with their effects being recorded.
— Finally what children learn in response to how they are taught should be noted on a regular basis. Some approaches to teaching, for example Precision Teaching (Raybould and Solity, 1982; Solity and Bull, 1987), advocate procedures which enable this to be done daily. Furthermore procedures are described within Precision Teaching which outline strategies for ensuring that teachers obtain systematic feedback on the effectiveness of their adopted teaching methods. The teacher using this or similar curriculum-related approaches is constantly evaluating children's learning to ensure that their contribution to the learning process is maximally effective.

The more frequently progress is monitored the better, as this increases the available information on which teaching decisions can be taken. The more frequently collected and detailed the records, the more reliable daily decisions made in the classroom become, with the teacher ultimately building up a much more comprehensive understanding of a child's needs and the best provision to meet those needs. Certainly the school will be gathering important data indicating the extent to which existing resources and provision are meeting a child's needs.

Aiming for the 'video' rather than the 'snapshot' also shifts the emphasis from merely looking at what children have learned at any moment in time, to seeing how quickly they are learning. Knowing how much children have learned is important but it is not sufficient; we also need to look at their rates of learning and the rate at which they are improving.

It will often be the case that a child who is thought to have a difficulty in learning, although behind peers in attainment levels, will actually be learning and improving at the same rate as other children. A continuous assessment procedure can ensure that this vital information is recorded.

Records therefore need to show what a child has learned in response to the various teaching arrangements provided.

Details of the Assessment-Through-Teaching for Children with Behaviour Problems

The information required has so far been related to children with learning difficulties. The same principles however, apply to where a child is presenting behaviour problems. The same comparisons with peers are helpful as are the details of the arrangements made to try and overcome the problems. As a result the following information should be prepared:
— a general description of the child's current behaviour, covering those aspects which are causing problems *but also* making detailed references to the areas where the child's behaviour is perfectly acceptable and appropriate;
— a comparison of the child's current behaviour with that of peers, again referring to areas where the comparisons are favourable and not just focusing on those where problems are experienced.

However, it is not always easy to estimate just how serious a child's disruptive behaviour is. Table 8.2 offers some guidelines to consider when assessing the seriousness of behavioural problems and are derived from Leach and Raybould (1977) and Bull and Solity (1987).

Initially, it is important to determine your own reactions to a child who is misbehaving. A teacher needs to look at why certain behaviour is seen as troublesome and unwanted. Many of us will be aware from our own experiences at school, that what was acceptable with one teacher may not have been with another. A teacher who is confronted with unwanted behaviour needs to look at the extent her personal attitudes and feelings might influence her perceptions of the child (*Step 1*).

A teacher also needs to be clear about precisely what a child is doing that is considered problematic. To describe a pupil as 'aggressive' or 'inconsiderate' will not necessarily convey a clear picture to the reader of the advice about what a child was *doing* to create this impression. It is preferable to be specific about what the child actually does that causes

Table 8.2
Steps for Assessing the Seriousness of a Child's Problem Behaviour

Step 1	Look at your own reactions to the child who is misbehaving.
Step 2	Define the behaviour which worries you (i.e. what does the child actually *do*?).
Step 3	Observe the frequency, duration and reasonableness of the behaviour which concerns you.
Step 4	Compare the child's behaviour (both acceptable and unacceptable) with that of his peers.
Step 5	Assess the effects of the behaviour of concern on the child's activities and those of others.
Step 6	Estimate other pupils' acceptance of the behaviour and the child.
Step 7	Try to identify relevant factors in the classroom environment that might be contributing to the child's behaviour.
Step 8	Find out how widespread the difficulties are.

concern (*Step 2*). For example a child may be seen as aggressive because she:

— pushes children in the dinner queue,
— runs into children in the playground and knocks them over,
— hits children in the classroom.

What the child does that is unwanted then needs to be observed over a period of time (*Step 3*). Some incidents whilst dramatic in nature may be a response to current circumstances which do not exist over a prolonged period. Therefore a child's behaviour should be observed to determine:

— how often it occurs
— its duration
— its reasonableness. For example, is it possible that the child's behaviour, although unwanted was actually an understandable response to the circumstances which may have prompted it?

The child's behaviour should be looked at carefully and compared to that of his peers (*Step 5*). Sometimes a child can get identified as a 'troublemaker' and then inevitably becomes the immediate focus of attention when misbehaviour occurs. This can lead to his being blamed for every disruptive incident when in fact other children are behaving in similar ways. So the question that needs answering is how different is the child's behaviour from that of his peers.

The effects of the unwanted behaviour should also be considered, in terms of how it influences the activities of other pupils and the extent to which it prevents the child concerned from completing her work or participating in the life of the school (*Step 5*). Not all misbehaviour will have equally serious or significant consequences for other children in the classroom. Similarly the unwanted behaviour has to be considered in the light of how other pupils view the child who misbehaves (*Step 6*). Some children who are perceived as disruptive are very much 'outsiders' as far as the rest of the children are concerned. On the other hand, some pupils are readily accepted members of the class group and have extremely positive relationships with peers.

In many cases, there may be factors existing within the classroom which contribute in some way to a child displaying unwanted behaviour (*Step 7*). These could be related to the lesson content (work may be too easy, or too difficult, or uninteresting), the child's position in the classroom (he may be too far away from the teacher and not hear everything that is being said), or the instructions for a particular activity could be too difficult and therefore misunderstood. Equally the child may be 'playing to the audience' and hoping for some reaction from peers or seeking the teacher's attention. For some children, any attention from the teacher, even when it arises through misbehaviour is better than no attention at all.

Finally, it is important to see just how widespread the unwanted behaviour is (*Step 8*). In how many different situations does it occur and with how many different people? What may be learned from the observation that the child responds well in one teaching situation as opposed to another?

These guidelines will help in formulating a comprehensive picture of the existing situation and the extent to which a child's behaviour can be managed with existing resources. The questions the guidelines address also need to be considered at the point when problems are first identified as they can help a teacher clarify precisely what the areas of difficulty are and provide a basis on which to intervene and alleviate the situation.

The steps taken to overcome a child's behaviour difficulties need to be carefully documented. The patterns of classroom organisation, choice of teaching methods and ways of responding to a pupil need to be noted and related to the child's behaviour and any changes that might occur. Again, modifications to any aspects of the child's learning environment need to be introduced systematically so their effects can be more clearly appraised.

A thorough account of the behaviour problems a child presents and the steps taken to overcome them has to be coupled with details of the child's academic progress, along the lines described in the previous section on collecting information on children seen as having a learning difficulty.

Consultations

Reference should also be made to any significant consultations that have taken place with other professionals such as educational psychologists, advisory teachers, speech therapists etc., together with details of outcomes and decisions taken.

Parents' Views

The Act gives parents the right to make independent submissions in writing to the LEA, either on their own or through an intermediary who may be an officer of the LEA. These are made available to teachers and other contributors to the procedure before their advice has to be submitted. Teachers may also wish to indicate in their advice what they understand the parents' opinions to be on their child's educational needs. This particular issue is considered in more detail in the next chapter, Working With Parents.

Attributing Sources

What a teacher learns about a child is a direct result of personal contact with that pupil together with discussions with colleagues, parents and other professionals. In compiling the advice it is important to clarify what the sources of information have been. The information presented should ideally be referenced to its origins, for example:
— the process of assessment-through-teaching,
— consultations with colleagues or other professionals,
— meetings with parents,
— some other source such as previous school records.

Distinguishing Between Facts and Opinion

When preparing advice, it is also important to make an *explicit* distinction between what might be regarded as fact and what could be viewed as opinion. Whilst to a philosopher there might be very little, if any difference between the two, it is we think relevant in the context of this chapter, to offer some working definitions.

When it comes to preparing advice, facts can be seen as information which can be supported by some form of data collected in the classroom or the wider school environment. Information based on data can be seen as 'objective' in the sense that the material from which it is derived is available for examination by others. The conclusions reached following a period of assessment-through-teaching can be evaluated through looking at the results of the assessment process.

Opinion, on the other hand, is information which is not supported by data. It is a point of view which will most probably be based on personal experience, which is the source of its validity, rather than being the result of a systematic investigation into the effects on a child's learning of different patterns of classroom organisation or choice of teaching or management approaches. We have little doubt that professional experience and judgement are important factors in helping a teacher respond to a child's needs. It is not a question of preferring fact to opinion or vice versa, but making it clear when writing advice *whether* the information presented is derived from a shared data base (in which case it can be viewed as factual) or whether it is the result of a personal opinion and judgement.

Normative Data

In Chapter 5, we commented on what we perceive to be the status of normative test data as a source of information on children's educational needs, together with some guidelines on selecting, administering and interpreting normative tests. In particular, we would urge that, when such test data is included in a school's written advice, results are clearly specified in the way we suggested, in order to *reduce any ambiguity or risk of misinterpretation by others*. However cautious and diligent the teacher has been in applying the test and in recording the results, there is always the danger that the reader of the report may seize upon a test score, possibly out of context, and jump to premature or unwarranted conclusions!

Test results do not have a meaning of their own, unrelated to the child's past or present educational experience. They do, however, have a habit of sticking in people's memories. It is important therefore to make your own interpretations of any results you choose to present. What conclusions do you feel you can reliably draw from the child's performance on the test? Do the results support your views of the child's needs or do they raise questions to be investigated further? Has the child made improvements in areas of the curriculum which are not reflected in the test scores obtained? How similar or difficult are the child's results compared with those obtained by his immediate peer-group within the school? What is the significance of the results for the teaching he should receive?

The results from normative tests therefore, when included in the school's advice, should be presented with considerable caution and qualification. Such tests have been used extensively in the past but as we have argued, their appeal probably outweighs their actual value in terms of the contribution they can make to an understanding of a child's educational needs.

Confidential Information

Through the course of preparing advice and consultations with others, it is likely that in some cases, highly personal information about the child or his family circumstances will come to light which will need treating with sensitivity. It might be felt that the implications of such information will have a significant bearing on the child's life both in and out of school. However, it is often difficult for a school to decide *whether* to include the information in the advice and *how* to present it. As a general rule, it is perhaps helpful to remember that the advice submitted by a school is termed the *educational* advice, thus placing the focus upon factors within the child's educational experience which have a direct bearing on his educational needs.

Should a teacher learn, for example, that a parent is the subject of criminal investigations, is suffering from a serious illness, or is in the middle of a marital breakdown, then it would be advisable to consult with the parent, and seek guidance on the matter. As a general rule information relating to the child or his family which is of a highly personal nature should probably only be included if:

— it can be seen to have a bearing on the child's educational needs, *and*
— the parents agree to its inclusion and how it is presented.

If it is considered that a child might be at risk socially, emotionally or physically, it would be prudent to consult an appropriate agency such as the School Psychological or Child Guidance Service, Social Services or Health Authority for general guidance on how to proceed.

Dealing With Disagreements

Through discussions with other professionals, colleagues, or parents there will be occasions when opinions differ regarding aspects of the child's assessment or descriptions of educational needs. It is made clear in Circular 1/83 that each professional assessing a child's educational needs, is responsible for the views that he or she advances. It is important therefore that the opinions included in the advice are the ones which a teacher feels are those based on her knowledge of the child and which emerge through the period of assessment. Procedures are laid down in the legislation to enable the LEA to try and resolve differences of opinion between professionals.

Similarly, where disagreements exist between a school and parents, these can be acknowledged in the advice and need not be ignored, dismissed, rejected or covered up. Handling differences of opinions with parents is a subject discussed in some detail in the next chapter. At this point we would wish to draw attention to the importance we attach to acknowledging what parents have to say, and referring to their views accurately and sensitively even where they are in conflict with those of the teacher or advice writer.

Differences of opinion emerging between teaching colleagues can also be included in the advice. If the views expressed are supported by relevant data then so much the better, but it might well be that in complex cases there is no single, easily identifiable answer to the questions being posed.

However, when looking at all the advice, the LEA might be able to obtain a more complete understanding of the child's needs when the views of the different professionals are available, than teachers or any individual professional can, when working on their own.

Whilst life might be seen to be less stressful when agreement is immediately forthcoming from all those involved in working with a child, this may in fact lead to an incomplete, possibly less helpful picture of the pupil being conveyed. Differences can be discussed and resolved at a later stage once individual opinions have been presented in a climate of honesty and mutual acceptance.

What Have You Learned?

The final preparatory step before actually writing the advice is to take a good look at the assembled information and decide what has been learned about the child. The questions to be answered relate to the identification of the child's needs and recommendations, on the basis of the completed assessment, about the most appropriate provision to meet those needs. This information then has to be put together in a coherent and readable way, so those reading the advice get a clear understanding of the results of the school's investigations into the child's educational needs.

WRITING THE ADVICE

The advice is likely to be read by many people, all of whom have had different levels of contact with the child and have varying levels of expertise in the field of special needs. To write, therefore, with any single reader in mind would be inappropriate. Possibly the most useful position is to imagine the reader as being intelligent and reasonable, but with little knowledge of either the child or special education.

The actual format of the advice might need to vary from child to child and so, as was stated in the introduction to this chapter, no definitive format will be offered.

A suggested checklist for advice has been issued by the DES (in Annex 1 of Circular 1/83). Our reluctance to recommend this format is based on the fact that it does, on the whole, invite comments and opinions derived from a rather 'static' view of the child from the administration of normative tests. Despite the content of the Act and Circular 1/83, and the positive interpretations we have offered, a very different view is also possible. This would adhere much more closely to what was described in Chapter 2, as the 'medical' model, whereby the assessment is largely psychometric and aimed at finding out what is 'wrong' with the pupil. The questions on the forms do not, in our view, encourage and provide space for the kind of information we are suggesting should be included, and that will help contribute to a comprehensive understanding of a child's needs. The checklist at the end of Circular 1/83 is seen as a suggested checklist only, and is presented as such by the DES. So while its categories may be relevant, the checklist does not lend itself readily to the type of continuous assessment emphasised as desirable in this book and the trying out of 'different approaches' referred to elsewhere in Circular 1/83 (Paragraph 11).

What we offer instead are some general guidelines within which to present the collected information on any child. Areas which we think should be considered are listed in Table 8.3.

Table 8.3
Areas to Consider When Writing Advice

Background information.
What the child has learned.
Comparison with peers.
Child's response to teaching.
Analysis of child's difficulties.
Comment on child's strengths.
Child's educational needs.
Provision available at present school to meet child's needs.
Provision required to meet child's needs.
Views of parents and child.

However, before writing the advice, it is important to provide a few essential details about the child along the following lines:

> Name of child
> Date of birth
> Chronological age
> Address
> School

This would be coupled with a heading to indicate that the document was the school's educational advice, on a child who it is thought may have special educational needs, and on whom an assessment has been completed. A further note stating that the advice was being submitted in accordance with the Educational (Special Educational Needs) Regulations (1983), and in compliance with Section 5 of the Education Act, might sound unnecessarily formal, but it will help the reader to appreciate immediately its status and relevance.

Background Information

The scene needs to be set for the reader of the advice, and a context provided in which the assessment took place. Appropriate details to include here would be:

> — the referring agency,
> — the reason for the referral,
> — a summary of the child's previous educational experiences, i.e. schools attended together with dates, etc.,
> — a summary of the assessment carried out to identify the child's

needs and the provision made available in school,
— an indication of the time scale over which the assessment has taken place,
— when and by whom it was first noticed that the child was experiencing difficulties.

Details of the Assessment-Through-Teaching

Some general information outlining the aims of the assessment period, together with an overview of the arrangements made to complete the assessment, would be a useful starting point. The specific details of the assessment can then be grouped under a number of different themes representing the data collected, which will be along the following lines;

— what the child had learned by the start of the assessment period,
— the arrangements made for teaching,
— the child's response to teaching,
— what the child had learned by the end of the assessment period,
— comparison of the child's rate of learning and attainment levels with that of peers.

The information presented would be a summary of the findings arising from the assessment, the aim being to make the information readily accessible and easy to understand. Information can be given added clarity by the use of tables summarising the main points to emerge during the assessment. Similarly graphs displaying aspects of the child's learning could help in highlighting specific areas for the reader. Any data that is important, but perhaps too technical or detailed for inclusion in the main body of the advice could be contained in an appendix. Such information could well be valuable in the event of parents appealing against the LEA's decision. The credibility and value of the teacher's advice could be determined in part during an appeal, by the extent to which the views expressed could be supported by data.

An analysis of the child's difficulties. Given the information to hand, the teacher's understanding of the nature of the child's difficulties is sought. This is an area where reference might well be made to consultations with professionals, if discussion has been helpful in leading to an understanding of the child's problems. However, the main source of information here will be the findings from the continuous assessment period.

An analysis of the child's strengths. Circular 1/83 emphasises the importance of commenting on the child's strengths as well as his difficulties. To focus exclusively on the latter could lead to a distorted picture of the child and his needs. An appropriate balance can be achieved by giving weight to an analysis and appreciation of the child's strengths.

Child's Educational Needs

As suggested in Chapter 4, an educational need can be best viewed as identifying the skills a child lacks which are important for him to learn. By the completion of the continuous assessment, it will be possible to determine just which skills the child still needs to be taught in order to achieve this aim. The extent to which the child's needs differ from those of the majority of peers in his class or year group will also be apparent.

It is important to stress at this point that it is not necessary for the school to decide whether or not the child's educational needs are *special educational needs*. The Act makes it clear that it is only the LEA that is required to make such a judgement. The school does not therefore need to find the means of determining whether a child's difficulties in learning are *significantly greater* than the majority of children of his age. Views expressed in this area by teachers are far more likely to be the result of administrative necessity, rather than the result of irrefutable fact. As we outlined in Chapter 6, judgements on this topic are, at best, based on experience, which may give them validity, but does not make them definitive.

Present School Provision

The present school provision and its capacity to meet the child's needs should be outlined. Again this is the expressed opinion of the school, and is based on professional judgement. However, the assessment procedure should have yielded sufficient data to lend considerable weight to the opinion expressed.

Provision Required to Meet the Child's Needs

The writer of the advice is also asked to offer a view on the most suitable provision to meet the child's needs. This information should be offered without reference to what is *actually* available, or likely to be available within the LEA. Therefore if it is felt that a particular form of provision is desirable, but not currently on offer by the LEA, then this should not prevent it from being recommended. However as Rodgers (1986b) shows, LEAs have exerted a certain amount of pressure on their employees to suggest only those forms of provision which can be provided. The reason for this is understandable in the light of government statements about the funding, or lack of it, for the implementation of the Act.

Nevertheless, we feel it important for those submitting advice, to draw the attention of the LEA to what is actually required by a child.

Only then will the LEA be in a position to determine that a particular type of provision, although presently lacking within the authority, is needed by an increasing number of pupils. This, at least, creates the opportunity for the LEA to consider the case for allocating or reallocating resources.

Equally, it is important that the parents can also feel that a teacher's recommendations about the appropriate form of provision for their child will be based on their professional judgement and knowledge of the child, and not constrained by the need to preserve the *status quo*.

Views of Parents

In particular, reference should be made to the discussions between the school and the parents regarding the child. Are the parents generally in agreement with the school's perceptions about the child's difficulties and needs? Is there partial agreement only; if so, how do their views differ? Are the parents' views totally at variance with those of the school? If so, what *are* their wishes and expectations?

It should be recognised that many parents may not choose to make their own representations to the LEA under the formal assessment procedure, as is their right. In which case, the school may be placed in a position to represent the parents' views on their behalf. This is a situation which clearly requires a high level of sensitivity and integrity on the part of the school staff and will be further discussed in Chapter 9.

SUMMARY

The 'advice' is the report written by teachers expressing their understanding and appreciation of a child's educational needs and the most suitable provision to meet those needs. Ideally, the advice will be based largely on the regular records that are already being compiled on children's progress and development. It should be valid, reliable, fair, comprehensive, readily understood and pass the acid test: 'would you like your child to be written about in this way?'

Appendix 2 presents a list of questions you might wish to apply when looking at an advice.

Chapter Nine

WORKING WITH PARENTS

INTRODUCTION

The chapter is very different in nature from preceding ones. Writing it has been the most difficult of all since it is about how we interact with people. This is probably best learned through experience, rather than from reading books. Whilst accepting this obvious limitation, we wish to raise some perennial issues that apply to the broad range of contact which teachers have with parents, not just those which occur in connection with the Act. It is also important to recognise that the issues exist when any professional works with parents, whether they are employed within the education department (e.g. educational psychologists) or outside (e.g. social workers, doctors, physiotherapists).

These issues, however, are inevitably brought into sharper focus when working with the parents of children who are seen to be experiencing difficulties at school. Additional strains could arise through the vulnerability felt by a parent at the suggestion that their child had a difficulty in learning. This is likely to place the parent-teacher relationship under additional tension through the feelings of frustration, apprehension, worry, guilt, disappointment being experienced by either party.

In this chapter we first look at the background to parent involvement in education and consider its importance. We then proceed to examine the settings in which parents and teachers might meet, look at how things could go wrong and offer some general principles for constructive parent–teacher relationships.

THE PRESENT CONTEXT FOR WORKING WITH PARENTS

Since the early 1980s many changes have taken place in the world of education. One of the most notable has been the increasing role given to parents in their children's education through various Acts of Parliament. These have sought to increase parental choice over which schools their children attend, given them increased participation on school governing bodies and offered them increased rights with respect to children with special needs. So the changes that have taken place in special education are not an isolated incidence of increased parental participation.

Furthermore, and apart from government legislation, parental involvement in children's education generally has been a growing area.

Articles in recent education journals and the education pages of the national press, have devoted a great deal of space to debating the effectiveness of parental contributions to their children's learning. (For a review see Topping and Wolfendale, 1985.) This then is the expanding context of parental involvement in children's education which has run parallel to their participation in special education.

HOW DOES THE ACT INVOLVE PARENTS?

The Act itself gives parents a greater say in what happens to their children should they have special educational needs than has hitherto been the case. The 'spirit' of the new legislation however is conveyed within Circular 1/83. For example, as was described in Chapter 7, parents are invited or required to participate at various decision-making stages of the statutory assessment procedure. Schools are exhorted to involve parents at the earliest possible opportunity in the assessment progress.

Assessment should be seen as a partnership between teacher, other professionals and parents.

Paragraph 6

Similarly when commenting on the gradual involvement of other professionals in the assessment process the Circular states:

The child's parents should be kept fully informed at every stage.

Paragraph 9

As well as encouraging parental participation at an early stage, the Act requires that parents be consulted before a formal, statutory assessment can be initiated.

Once it is under way they can make independent representations to the LEA, informing them of their own views about the educational needs of their children. Similarly, all the professionals submitting advice have to consult parents, and take into account their opinions. Also, where it is feasible, parents are allowed to attend assessments of their children. This, of course, presupposes that the assessment is a one-off event, conducted on a single, or limited number of occasions and is likely to be associated with a normative and psychometric orientation to identifying children's educational needs.

Where the assessment is continuous, it is less practical for parents to attend in the way envisaged. However, the principle of parent involvement is equally valid and can still be upheld, but within a slightly different set of circumstances. Instead of being present at the 'assessment', parents can be kept informed of their child's progress and participate with teachers in establishing and working towards agreed educational goals.

Parents are sent copies of all the advice when a provisional statement is written and they have to approve its contents and recommendations before it can become substantive. Where they are not satisfied with the provision it makes, they can appeal to an LEA committee, and ultimately to the Secretary of State for Education if necessary.

Parents also have the right to appeal against a decision in the event that the LEA decides not to make special educational provision for a child. The crucial difference between the two instances where appeals are possible is that in the former, the Secretary of State is empowered to direct the LEA to change some aspect of its decision. In the latter this is not the case, and the most that parents can expect is that the Secretary of State would ask the LEA to reconsider its decision; it cannot be directed to change.

Implications for Parents and Schools

It is clearly one thing to give parents increased rights, and quite another to *enable* them to exercise those rights. An obvious criticism of the legislation is that although it provides a sequence of steps to be followed to ensure that parents are consulted and informed of their rights, it can be interpreted in different ways by LEAs. This has meant that in some cases LEA documentation has been overwhelming, and not always sufficiently clear to inform parents of their rights in a way that can be easily understood. So whilst LEAs have been able to keep within the law, many parents may not have been aware of the role they are now able to play. A report prepared by Rodgers (1986a) illustrates this point and documents the way different LEAs have responded to the Act.

The Act has led to a marked increase in the literature now available for parents informing them of their rights, for example Newell (1983). There are also a large number of voluntary bodies and pressure groups that are actively providing information and advice for parents to enable them to exercise their rights and secure the provision they may feel is most appropriate for their children. That parents have had to set up such groups can be seen as a direct result of their appreciation that as far as their children have been concerned, there have on occasions been a conflict, and clash of interests between the needs of the LEA and the needs of the child. As Rodgers (1986a) indicated, it could be naive to think that LEAs are *always* acting in the best interests of the child.

The situation, and the developing role of parents, can also create difficulties for a school. Teachers, as emplyees of the LEA, may feel obliged to write advice along lines which are in keeping with LEA practices and so do not cause any embarrassment. Such advice may not represent the best interests of the child or the opinions of the parents.

Of course, the reverse of this situation could arise when the advice offered represents parental opinions, but perhaps makes recommendations that cannot easily be met by existing LEA provision or is not within the bounds of current policy. This highlights the dilemma which can face teachers when carrying out their assessment of a child's needs and preparing advice.

PARENTS AND TEACHERS: WORKING TOGETHER

It is clear to us that the provisions of the Act can only operate effectively and fairly, when the 'spirit' of the Act is observed. This is especially so in a school's relationship with parents. Circular 1/83 states:

> **Close relations should be established and maintained with parents and can only be helped by frankness and openness on all sides.**
> **Paragraph 6**

How can this be achieved? The type of relationship that develops between a school and a child's parents will in part be determined by the perceptions formed by parents of teachers' sincerity, understanding and competence. Where parents trust and feel confident about their child's teachers and the school he attends, they will be more certain that their views are being considered and that the child's needs are being given priority, in preference to any circumstantial considerations.

Where a positive relationship exists between parents and teachers, parents will in our view, inevitably be taking a fuller part in their child's education. They will be involved at an early stage in the assessment, be aware of the procedures being followed and possibly be contributing to the negotiation of educational goals. Parents are likely to feel more comfortable in offering and sharing information with teachers, which might well lead to a more thorough understanding and appreciation of their child's needs.

Schools have therefore to work towards establishing a positive relationship with parents in an atmosphere of mutual trust and acceptance. Whilst this is an aim that many would share, it is not always readily attained and a number of factors can prevent it from being achieved.

When parents and teachers come together over a child experiencing difficulties in school, both parties can be seen to have legitimate, though essentially different, interests and concerns. For the parents, they have obvious blood ties and will naturally be anxious about any problems their child is perceived to be experiencing at school.

Society places many expectations upon parents, which they will inevitably feel compelled to fulfil to some extent. A typical reaction among many teachers on hearing that a pupil is having difficulties at school, is to raise questions about the child's 'home background'. Parents may therefore feel they are under the microscope when they learn of any difficulties, and are likely to react in a way which maintains their own perceptions of themselves, the family environment they have provided and their child. The starting position for the parent could therefore be a defensive one, if they either feel, or pick up the suggestion that they may be 'to blame' in some way.

The source of teachers' concern arises from their professional responsibilities. They have the task of developing children's educational and social competence, and should a pupil fail to progress in these areas in the way that had been hoped, it is likely that a teacher will be sensitive to the suggestion that she has failed to do his job properly. As we discussed in Chapter 2, more traditional approaches to assessment could be seen as one response to this criticism, by locating the source of failure firmly within the child and not the teacher or educational programme. Now the situation is not quite as clear cut, as teachers are being asked to look increasingly at aspects of the teaching process, classroom environment and their interactions with children that may have been the cause of children failing. The teacher too, may therefore be feeling defensive when meeting with parents.

It is important to recognise that although parents and teachers have valid reasons for their reactions to a child who is failing and may have some common interests, their respective positions are *not equivalent*, nor do they necessarily imply common goals.

Areas of Contact Between Parent and Teachers

Parents and teachers come into contact in a number of different situations and on numerous occasions during the school year: open evenings, jumble sales, school plays and concerts, Christmas festivities, sports day etc. These are, however, all characterised by being initiated by the school rather than by parents. It is the school who decides when these take place, although parents may be consulted and their wishes considered. Increasingly, schools are opening their doors and welcoming contributions from parents during the school day, through their willingness to listen to children read and generally assist in the classroom. Even so, it is the school that usually determines the form, frequency and timings of this contact.

Meetings usually only take place outside these set times when either a parent or teacher is concerned about some aspect of the child's education, and wants to discuss this with the other party. Again, it is far more likely that the school will initiate a meeting of this type.

There are a number of reasons why teachers might request a meeting with parents when it appears that a child is experiencing difficulties. Sometimes one party or the other leaves the meeting feeling dissatisfied, but not always able to specify the reason for this. There are several common 'setting events' which may lead to miscommunication or friction between parents and teachers:

— parents or teachers may feel defensive if they suspect they are being blamed for what is regarded as the 'child's failure';

— they may hold different perceptions of the child;

— either party may be unsure of what the child has said about the other, in relation to either the school or home environments, and may be uncertain about whether a positive or negative image is being conveyed;

— problems could be compounded by parents' experiences of their own schooling, especially where these had been negative;

— a frequently expressed view in staff rooms is that it is always the parents you want to see most that do not come to parent evenings. One possible reason for this is that the children of these parents are often the ones experiencing the difficulties. In the past, typically much of what is said at these parent-teacher meetings about the child is negative and focuses on where the pupil is failing. Where this is the case parents would be justifiably apprehensive and recalcitrant about such meetings;

— the initial overtones from a school to the parents inviting them to a meeting can easily be a source of anxiety. Letters which appear out of the blue with an invitation to attend a meeting at a designated time and place, but which either do not specify the purpose or do so ambiguously, can create uncertainties and would lead a parent to feel guarded. Anyone receiving a similar type of letter from a bank manager would be able to identify with parents' feelings on these occasions.

A meeting which occurs in any of the above circumstances, is in danger of failing to reach a mutually satisfactory outcome. Since such circumstances create generally negative expectations on the part of the participants, and place them on guard, neither parents or teachers are likely to address the very points the meeting was called to discuss. The issues will get lost as individual corners and perspectives are protected.

There are several possible intentions for holding meetings with parents when a child is experiencing difficulties. Some common ones are:

— to express concern,

— to seek information,

— to convey information,

— to seek to establish parental participation in the child's learning.

It is salutary to look at each intention in turn and see how it might go wrong, when either the teacher or parent brings thoughts, feelings and perceptions to the meeting which are not fully disclosed. What appears to be happening on the surface is not what is actually happening when the interactions are examined more closely. This would not represent a deliberate attempt to deceive, but the result of being insufficiently aware of how what is said, is *received* from a different perspective. You might know what you intend to say, but is that what is actually said, and what sense might somebody else make of it?

Head: *I think I handled that really well.*

Expressing concern. A teacher's intention to express concern to the parents of a child experiencing difficulties at school seems very laudable. Parents will want to know how their children are progressing especially if there are difficulties and teachers will feel responsible for keeping them informed. However, this needs to be set in the context of the usual pattern of contact between parents and teachers to be fully appreciated.

As we have already discussed, the contact between many parents and teachers is often intermittent, and is usually confined to parent evenings or other scheduled occasions. Of course for some parents this is not the case and they are able to meet their children frequently from school, and so may well be in the fortunate position of being engaged in a regular dialogue with a teacher. In either event, for a parent to hear for the first time that their child is experiencing difficulties may well come as something of a shock. Parents are rarely, if ever, ready to receive this news even if their relationship with teachers in the school is very positive.

The intention to express concern is understandable but needs to be considered in the light of the way the information is presented and the effect it has on parents. What are the parents supposed to do with this information? What sense will they make of it? What would you want them to do with it? As we see it, the most likely effect on parents will be to increase their anxieties and lead them to worry about their child's progress. Being told that your child is not learning or is a constant disruptive influence on the rest of the class, can only lead to parental concerns increasing.

The information when expressed in this form does not offer parents a solution to the problem. They are not being invited to take part in a constructive dialogue to see how goals can be established jointly, and worked for co-operatively. Merely expressing concern, without trying to negotiate a solution to the difficulties, may result in the teacher feeling better but does little for the parents, because they are usually powerless to effect any direct changes to overcome the difficulties in the classroom.

In effect, what may be actually happening is that the teacher is 'leaving the problem' with the parent. The teacher may feel that his professional duty has been fulfilled but the parent is left in an increasingly anxious state without being offered scope to change the situation.

Expressing concern is valid and reasonable only when coupled with constructive discussions about possible strategies to overcome the presenting difficulties. When this is done, the stated aims are much more likely to be achieved, as they provide the starting point for some form of positive intervention. Parents are less likely to worry and feel anxious when they can appreciate that steps are being taken to help their child learn or develop appropriate patterns of behaviour.

Seeking information. It is frequently thought that by inviting parents to school and asking them about the situation at home, that information will be forthcoming that will help in dealing with the difficulties experienced at school. If we start with the example of a child who is having trouble in learning to read, what information could parents offer that would help alleviate the situation at school? If parents are asked what they do at home, the responses that they can actually give are fairly constrained. They are not likely to say that they are not interested in their child's reading, that they could not care less about the progress being made, that they do not encourage their child at home. Equally, they are not likely to say 'nothing, that's why we send him to school'.

Questions of this type will most probably elicit a highly predictable, and socially acceptable answer. The majority of parents are likely to say that they listen to their child read, care about his progress and help whenever possible.

The effect could be similar when a child is misbehaving at school. The parent's responses may also be entirely predictable and are likely to follow one of two lines. The first could be a form of denial: that there were no problems at home and everything was fine. Where would this leave the teacher? If she suspected the parent was not being truthful, she could hardly accuse the parent of dishonesty. Alternatively, it may lead to the teacher feeling defeated or undermined. The inference to be made is that, as the teachers are the only ones apparently faced with the difficulties, it must be something to do with them and and the way they are trying to teach the child in the classroom.

On the other hand, the parents could acknowledge that they were also experiencing some behaviour problems at home. Sometimes when this happens, rather than leading to a clearer understanding of how to proceed in the future, both teacher and parents may become locked into a dialogue along the lines of: 'Isn't it awful; do you know what he does?' Stories are exchanged indicating how troublesome the child's behaviour can be. At the end, parent and teacher may feel a little better, but only temporarily. It can be heartening to learn that you are not the only one in the same boat but such feelings quickly give way to ones of apprehension about how to overcome the difficulties being experienced. Exchanging stories of dreadful deeds does not lead to constructive solutions or positive ways of proceeding.

Again, seeking information, while ostensibly worthwhile and valid is not likely to achieve what was hoped. Of course there may be occasions when parents perceive events at home to be having a disturbing effect on their child and are worried that it may affect him at school. However, when this happens, and if parents feel it is significant, they are likely to visit school and volunteer the information. Clearly though, this will only happen where positive home–school relationships have been built up over a period of time. If parents do not feel comfortable in offering information on their own, it is extremely unlikely that they will do so when questioned by a teacher.

Conveying information. In principle, conveying information to parents and keeping them up to date on aspects of their child's education is desirable. The notion of conveying information carries with it the understanding that parents are given *factual details* of their child's education and progress. However, it is often coupled with expressing concern as well.

A typical scenario is where parents are invited to school to see the headteacher because a child is being disruptive in school. The head promises disgruntled staff who have grown weary with handling the child, that he will put the parents in the picture and sort everything out.

The head, after the opening pleasantries, presents the parents with a catalogue of incidents, detailing the time, place and nature of each misdemeanour. This can all be described accurately as conveying information. The story usually ends with the head expressing his personal concerns and representing the staff's corporate view which is also one of concern. In an extreme case, the parents might be told that if the misbehaviour does not stop immediately, there will be no alternative to suspension. The head returns to the staff room letting everyone know that the child's parents have been given the facts, are aware of the situation and the outcomes if the misbehaviour continues. Such a head may consider that he does not have difficulty in dealing with parents, but is it possible that parents may have difficulties in dealing with this type of head?

Where does a series of events like this leave the parents? They are likely to react in one of two ways. They will either feel worried and anxious but unable to do anything. Or they will feel angry and frustrated and may displace their feelings on the child when he gets home, on each other, or possibly on a teacher on another occasion.

Conveying information and giving feedback to parents is a necessary part of the teaching process. What needs to be looked at carefully is what the purpose is and how this going to be communicated to parents. What is wanted from parents? What are they expected to do with the feedback they receive? How will they react to it?

In the normal course of events where a child is progressing satisfactorily these issues would not be such sensitive areas. However, when a child is experiencing difficulties, the scene carries different and potentially more hurtful consequences for its participants.

Establishing parental participation in children's learning. Parental involvement in children's learning in now relatively well established in the field of special education. Educational psychologists and teachers of severely mentally or physically handicapped children have run projects over a number of years to involve parents actively in their children's learning. More recently these projects have been extended into ordinary schools and tended to concentrate on improving children's reading. Increasing attention has turned to all children and not just those who have had difficulties, and many initiatives have been reported to indicate the effectiveness of parental participation (Topping and

Wolfendale, 1985; Jackson and Hannon, 1981; Hewison *et al.*, 1982).

We do not wish to dispute the validity of these projects or question the research findings or methodological approaches adopted. Instead we want to consider the position of parents in the light of such a tidal wave of enthusiasm welcoming their involvement in children's learning. Parents have always been seen as important contributory factors in determining children's progress at school through the attitudes they hold about education and the support they give their children. 'Good parents' have always been involved and conscientiously listened to their children read at home or tested them on their sight reading from the flash cards in a 'word tin'. Now their role is being taken further as they are encouraged to participate in more formally organised, schoolbased reading projects.

Where does this leave the parent? What new pressures are being placed on them? What are the new perceptions of the 'good parent'? Can a parent say 'No'?

This appears to be the significant issue. Can a parent decide not to participate in a parental involvement project without any negative implications? Can they still be regarded as supportive, caring parents if they do not want to take part in a home/school reading project? What should be the response to a parent who said, 'Look I work hard during the day. I don't get home till 5.45 and after cooking the dinner I'm absolutely whacked. There are other things I want to do with the children than listen to them read. Anyway they get enough of that at school, it's your job to teach them to read. That's why I pay my rates. If they're not learning quickly maybe it's because of the way you're teaching them'.

Would parents articulating these views be seen to be neglecting their parental responsibilities? Might they be seen as unsupportive and uninterested in their child's education? When parents are informed of a parent-involvement project, and invited to take part, is it a genuine invitation, or a demand? Can they refuse and say no, without their being any negative repercussions? We would see it as vital that parents have a genuine choice and can legitimately decline the invitation without their role as parents being impugned. Otherwise they may feel trapped and pressurised into participating when they do not wish to do so.

Each of the above examples illustrates the importance of trying to appreciate the listener's point of view. Table 9.1 summarises the issues raised. No teacher would deliberately set out to place parents in situations where thet may feel trapped, anxious, helpless, etc. But it can certainly be an unfortunate, even though unintended outcome of meetings initiated by teachers (as well as other professionals) to discuss with parents a child's difficulties in school. It is therefore important that teachers 'tune in' to what sense parents are making of the meeting. So far we have looked at some ostensible aims for meeting with parents

Table 9.1
Reasons for Seeing Parents

Reason for calling meeting	Purpose	Possible inadvertent effects on parents
To express concern	Important that parents 'know'	'Left with' the problem
	Sense of duty	Angry
	Thought parents would want to know	Helpless
	Let parents know situation cannot continue	
To seek information from parents	Teacher wants to understand the situation better	Trapped
		Anxious
		Helpless
		Implied dishonesty
Convey information	If strictly factual then usually acceptable but often involves expressing concern as well	Anxious
		Angry
Parental participation	Gaining parents' co-operation	Trapped
		No way out without feeling criticised

and some possible underlying messages that may be transmitted to parents. We now wish to draw attention to those aspects of a teacher's *approach* to interviewing which may also inadvertently undermine the aims of a meeting.

Problems in Interviewing

People come to meetings with a range of previous experiences. Attitudes, values, personalities and patterns of behaviour are well established and all have a bearing on the ensuing interaction. We cannot demand how others should behave in a meeting and clearly cannot insist that they are open, honest and forthcoming in the way we might wish them to be. As interviewers, however, we are responsible for our own behaviour and for being aware of whether the way we communicate reflects our own attitudes, anxieties and opinions.

There are many ways in which teachers can reveal the areas in which they feel less than comfortable by the way an interview is conducted. The following are examples.

Asking too many questions. This may derive from the teacher's anxiety and can prevent the parents giving information at their own pace. The teacher wants to get to a solution quickly and so may deliver a series of questions, which are often phrased in a way to confirm the teacher's own impressions, rather than get the parents' view of the situation.

Asking closed questions. There is a danger also in phrasing questions in such a way as to elicit only a 'Yes' or 'No' response. For example: 'Are you concerned about X's behaviour at home?' A series of such questions can sound like an interrogation and is likely to have the effect of inhibiting or shutting down the flow of discussion. In contrast, open-ended questions beginning with what? how? where? and why? are more likely to facilitate the parents' contribution.

Filling the silences. Parents may need time to collect their thoughts and formulate an answer to the question. A question could prompt parents to look at events in a different way and they will need space to consider any new perspective on the problems which emerge. The teacher, through breaking the silence after asking a question, may again be reflecting his own uncertainties in the desire to get answers quickly, while at the same time interrupting and inhibiting the parent.

Proposing quick solutions. By proposing quick solutions, the teacher may be undermining the collaborative nature of parent-teacher interactions and pre-empting the parents' contribution to developing constructive ways of managing a pupil's difficulties. It could also be seen by parents as implying that what they think is not sufficiently important to lead to an understanding of their child's needs. Quick solutions also reflect the teacher's uncertainties in several ways. Not knowing why a child is failing creates its own anxieties which may be temporarily relieved by providing immediate explanations. Equally, where the teacher is feeling threatened or vulnerable, offering solutions may be seen as an attempt to demonstrate to the parent their expertise and control of the situation.

Interrupting the conversation. Whilst it is not always easy to predict the demands that are going to be made on a teacher during the course of a meeting with parents, answering the telephone, interruptions from outside or consulting with someone, looking up a reference, may give a number of messages to parents. They might infer that their meeting does not rank very highly in the teacher's list of priorities if so many interruptions are allowed. It might also be seen that there are aspects of the interview which the teacher is finding uncomfortable.

Focusing on areas which are most familiar. A parent may raise a number of issues during a conversation, some of which the teacher has previous experience and knowledge and others of which he does not. On these occasions there is a tendency to ignore areas which are unfamiliar and possibly of a more emotional nature and to concentrate on factors which are more familiar. This can also leave parents feeling that they have not managed to convey their side of the picture as what they are saying is effectively being dismissed by the teacher, who does not pursue these matters further.

Telling parents not to worry and that everying will be all right. Through the 'advice' a teacher gives, she is often saying more about her own reactions to a difficulty and the ways she would deal with it, rather than responding to and reflecting the parents' concerns. The teacher may respond to the situation by 'not worrying' but to advise the parents along these lines is to dismiss and minimise the very natural feelings they may be experiencing. The parent may then feel 'abnormal' or 'neurotic' whereas their reaction may be entirely justified and the one most people would experience under similar circumstances. The net outcome for parents very often is to cover up their natural reactions and present a view of themselves which the teacher can deal with and not feel uncomfortable about.

Telling parents not to be upset. This is a further example of how a teacher can indicate what she feels is the most appropriate way of responding to the situation. Getting upset or crying may be seen as too emotional or irrational, far better to 'pull yourself together' and deal with the problem logically than become worried and distressed. Again, a parent can be left feeling unsupported and overly emotional by failing to adopt what the teacher sees as a rational approach.

Making unrealistic proposals. A desire to appear competent, powerful and helpful can be expressed through promising more than can be realistically provided. Complex, troubling problems rarely have simple solutions. It may be more facilitative for the teacher to admit to his own uncertainty or puzzlement and 'think aloud' with the parents. By acknowledging the uncertainty of the situation, the teacher is more likely to be able to enjoin the parents in generating some possible ways forward.

Asking clever questions. By 'clever' questions we mean the sort of questions which leave the parents at some disadvantage (i.e where the teacher and parent are in a 'one up, one down' relationship). Clever questions may suggest that the teacher thinks of himself as a psychotherapist and wants to identify the underlying causes of the child's difficulties. Such an approach to questioning could undermine the notion of parents as equal partners in the education of their children through accentuating the teacher's need to feel in control, insightful and knowledgeable. The parent is then left feeling defensive and threatened.

It is natural for a teacher to want to help a parent understand a problem in as much depth as possible, but it is important for the teacher to recognise the boundaries of his or her own area of expertise and appreciate where it can be helpful, and acknowledge when the best source of assistance can come from elsewhere. In teaching, as in other professions, it is as important to be aware of what you *do not* know, as what you do know.

Using jargon. In Chapter 8, we discussed some of the problems associated with using jargon in written reports. It is salutary to bear in mind that what we, as professionals, often think of as commonplace or vernacular, is still jargon to parents and best avoided. Its use may reflect the need to appear superior and knowledgeable and, possibly, the extent to which the teacher feels defensive. The parent is likely to feel intimidated and less of a 'partner' in the discussion.

Each of these examples illustrates the ways in which the teacher's approach can affect the interview with parents. Our observations are not intended as criticisms of teachers and should not be seen as implying that such effects are in any way deliberate. Quite clearly they are not, and that is part of the problem. We are often very aware of issues which make us feel anxious and less than adequate. What is much more difficult to appreciate is how we may communicate these issues inadvertently to others.

Our aim is to increase awareness of their potentially disadvantaging effect on parents, who as we already pointed out, are likely to be feeling apprehensive on being invited to school to discuss their child's difficulties. No teacher would wish to leave parents feeling dismissed, defensive, anxious, powerless, undervalued or intimidated. When everything is running smoothly and children are making satisfactory progress, we are far less likely to look closely at the nature of interactions with parents and explore areas of potential miscommunication. When talking to parents whose children are having problems, these issues are highlighted and require our close attention.

PRINCIPLES OF EFFECTIVE COMMUNICATION

The principles presented here have emerged consistently in the fields of counselling and inter-personal psychology as being those which can most successfully facilitate effective interactions between individuals who find themselves in positions similar to those of teachers talking with parents. We recognise that the professional relationship between counsellor and client, doctor and patient, is not directly analogous to that between teacher and parent. One obvious difference is that teacher and parent are ostensibly communicating about a third party, the child, about whom they have different interests and concerns. Clearly, the teacher is not normally expected to be in a professional counselling relationship with parents. If we desire to work in a genuine partnership with parents, however, it is important to take account of the general principles which we go on to describe as they are crucial to developing effective communications.

There are also a number of difficulties in writing about these principles. To become effective as a communicator with parents takes time and is learned through experience. Merely to read about the principles and not see their effects in practice, whether successful or otherwise, could lead to an oversimplification of the entire process. At the same time, it can appear manipulative that the desired attitudes will be conveyed through learning the appropriate skills. We are reminded of the training which fast-food operatives get in saying 'Have a nice day!'. This is perhaps a small risk, as simply knowing what to do at an intellectual level can never guarantee success at an experiential level. But the process of effective communication can appear somewhat cold and calculating when presented in the written form.

Despite these reservations, our aim here is to convey something of the way in which, we believe, teachers can and do communicate effectively with parents.

Working Effectively with Parents

Working effectively with the parents of children who experience difficulties is determined, in part, by the feelings and attitudes held by a teacher about the parents. These have been discussed by Cunningham and Davis (1985). We would like to highlight three fundamental aspects of effective relationship-building. They are:
— respect,

— empathy,
— genuineness.
How are these aspects *conveyed* to parent?

Conveying respect. This starts from an acceptance that parents and teachers are equal partners or collaborators in the education of their children. Each party has different responsibilities, and a meeting where parents recognise they are seen as equals will help create the desired climate which will establish a positive basis for discussion.

Respect is also conveyed by what is known as *active listening*. Listening is often thought of as being a passive activity. Talking is active and can therefore be observed. But how do you know someone is listening? Initially, by being courteous and remembering important details from previous encounters. Then during the conversation, looking involved, an attitude demonstrated non-verbally through posture, facial expression and eye contact. It is frequently said that actions speak louder than words and the non-verbal aspects of behaviour often convey more information than the verbal component. Some specific instances of how this happens will be discussed later in this chapter.

Active listening also involves *summarising* what has been said so that the teacher can check that she has understood what the parents actually intended to say. This can also be helpful to the parents in giving them a 'reflection' of their own point of view.

To get a clear impression of what parents are saying may also involve:
—*seeking information* where uncertainty exists about what is meant,
—*asking for concrete* examples where parents describe specific instances which illustrate the point they have been making,
—*noticing inconsistencies* and feeding these back to parents.
Individuals use language differently and it can sometimes be the case that a parent uses language and expressions which are unfamiliar to us. Where parents appear to be contradictory or inconsistent, it is helpful to clarify whether we have misunderstood through the way we have interpreted what parents have said or whether the parents have conveyed conflicting messages. However, pointing out an inconsistency may be read as challenging by parents especially where they have been unaware of the contradiction, so this must be done sensitively and its success would be determined in part by the quality of the relationship already established.

Respect is also conveyed by the way parents are treated generally in the overtures to a meeting. What was the nature of the initial contact? How was a time negotiated with parents? How were parents received on arriving at school? Did the meeting start promptly? Were they offered a cup of tea?

It is often many of the 'little things' that do most to enhance or damage a parent's perception of the school. To refer to them as the 'little things' may seem paradoxical given their potential influence. However, as they are the context, rather than the substance of the meeting, their impact can often be overlooked. Taken on their own they may not appear particularly significant, but their combined effect can be setting the scene for a positive parent–teacher relationship and help the parents appreciate that their presence is valued and worth making an effort for.

Parents can also appreciate that their contributions to discussion are respected by teachers *accepting* what they say *without passing judgement*. A parent when once asked what she would most like to be able to give to her children said, 'the benefit of hindsight'. It is always easy to be wise after the event, spot the mistakes of others and think that you would not have handled things like that. But that is never the case. No one gets it right all the time and to be aware of this will help in accepting what parents say and how they behave. Parents may feel they have to be 'perfect' in how they bring up their children, especially when talking to teachers about the problems children are seen to be experiencing. However, no parent or teacher for that matter, will ever be perfect; it is an unrealistic, unattainable goal. Likewise, the teacher who can accept being *good enough* will be more likely to regard parents as good enough and accept, non-judgementally what the parents say or do.

The important distinction to recognise here is between *acceptance* and *agreement*. It is not expected that teachers will necessarily agree with all the parents' actions, but may accept that they were doing their best, at the time, under the conditions they found themselves to be in.

Conveying empathy. Establishing empathy is where we try to put ourselves in someone else's shoes to understand something of how they might be looking at the world. Empathy is conveyed not so much by saying to parents 'I understand' or 'I can imagine how you feel' but by reflecting to parents that their position is acknowledged and appreciated. The former statements do not indicate that the listener has fully recognised precisely how a speaker is feeling. These words can be spoken in response to almost any distressing disclosure and so may carry less weight, and in some circumstances could be received as platitudinous or dismissive.

What is important is demonstrating to parents that what they have said, *has actually been heard*. This is conveyed in two ways. Our non-verbal behaviour (e.g. posture, eye contact) can demonstrate that we are actively listening and involved in what the parent is saying. How we respond verbally is equally important and it complements non-verbal behaviour.

For us to be empathic, what we say to parents must in some way convey our appreciation of *how they are feeling*. For example, a parent might report that she had frequently been told by different teachers that her child was experiencing difficulties in school. When she had enquired about what she could do to help, she was told not to worry and that the child would probably 'grow out of it'. Intuition might lead us to anticipate some feelings likely to be aroused in the parent. One way to illustrate to the parent that you have understood her predicament could be to say something like: 'It seems like the explanations you were offered left you feeling frustrated, perhaps even helpless'. A comment such as this shows both active listening and an understanding of the parents' feelings. The parent then has an opportunity to indicate whether the interviewer's perception of how it affected her was accurate.

What frequently happens, as this example illustrates, it that the parent reports a series of events, without necessarily stating overtly how this influenced them emotionally. What the teacher reflects in his comments, is the feelings this may have given rise to. To achieve this the teacher must be putting something of himself in the discussion and anticipating how he might feel under similar circumstances.

In coneying empathy therefore, the teacher:
— actively listens to parents.
— feeds back the feelings they sense parents have experienced in response to the presented circumstances, which parents often described as a series of events rather than as their emotional responses.
— draws on what his own feelings might be if placed in similar circumstances.

Whilst it is tempting to say 'I understand' or 'I know how you feel', such comments do not convey the same level of appreciation of how parents might be perceiving events and feeling about them. They do not leave room for the parents to confirm or elaborate their feelings.

There are occasions when it is appropriate to disclose to parents that similar events have had the same effect on you. Equally, although you may never have been in the same position as parents, but have on occasions experienced the same *feelings,* this can be fed back to them, for example through such a comment as 'Yes there have been times when I've felt frustrated and helpless and didn't know how to deal with a situation'.

Being genuine. One important way in which genuineness is conveyed is through the interviewer being prepared to disclose something of his own feelings when this is relevant and supportive. Appropriate self-disclosure is not a matter of exchanging anecdotes, for example: 'If you think you've got problems, let me tell you about some of mine'. Its purpose is to indicate to parents that you have appreciated how they are feeling, and are letting them know that it is *all right* to experience those feelings as natural and acceptable reactions to the prevailing circumstances.

When we perceive things are going wrong, and look at others, there is a tendency to think we are unjustified in reacting as we have done, that everyone else would handle it better. We may imagine that others would think us silly or stupid for feeling as we do and that we may therefore be judged negatively. But there is much to recommend the aphorism, 'A trouble shared is a trouble halved'. Anyone who has discussed a problem with someone else may well have been aware of a sense of relief afterwards, like a great load being removed from our shoulders. Indicating you have experienced similar emotions to a parent, can help them accept their feelings and appreciate that the listener is 'human'.

The parallel situation for teachers is the frequently caricatured scenario whereby in some schools the classroom doors close at 9.00 a.m. only for the teacher to reappear at lunchtime and after school at 3.30 p.m., but never discussing what happens during the intervening period. To admit that things are not going well or that problems are being experienced is seen to be an admission of failure. The tendency is to think that everyone else is competent except us. However, when discussions about these areas do take place, it can be reassuring to find that others are experiencing the same difficulties and the solutions can be sought collaboratively rather than individually. So it is with parents. They will feel less threatened and vulnerable to know the teacher to whom they are talking is sensitive to, and aware of, how they are feeling.

Genuineness can also be displayed more effectively when a teacher is aware of her own attitudes and values in relation to the topic being discussed. We have already discussed how a positive interaction between teacher and parents may be affected detrimentally by the personal issues which a teacher may bring to a discussion. When a teacher is aware of these issues, it is far more likely that the ensuing interaction will be productive. A different form of self-disclosure could therefore involve drawing a parent's attention to their own attitudes to the subject under discussion.

For example, when discussing the prospects for integrating a child with special needs, it might be appropriate for a teacher to *declare* his own views on this topic, rather than imply a position of impartiality. So where a teacher is strongly in favour of segregated special education their starting position to a parent could be: 'I want to begin by saying that I'm personally in favour of the form of provision available in special schools. However, although I believe this to be the case, I will try to offer advice which is in the best interest of your child, irrespective of my own personal convictions'. We would see this as valid, and preferable to attempting to maintain an apparently 'value free' position which could be construed as being less honest. A disclosure of this kind would contribute to the parents' perception of the teacher as genuine.

Our genuineness is also reflected in how we articulate 'the problem' to the parents. In reality, whatever the reasons for the problems which a child may present in the classroom, it is the teacher who is faced with the difficult task of managing and alleviating those problems. If the problems are such that the teacher feels angry or defeated, no productive purpose will be served by acting out those feelings in the interview with the parents. At the same time, it would be less than genuine to pretend that the feelings were not there. Perhaps one way this can be acknowledged and presented to parents is through saying, 'At the moment I am having difficulties working with X. Things just don't seem to be going well and this is what I would like to discuss with you. I'd like to see if there is any way you can help me understand the situation better; perhaps we could work together to improve it'.

Non-verbal behaviour reflects how the teacher is perceived by the parent. Genuineness will be conveyed by the appropriate non-verbal signals and by those matching the verbal content of the communication. Where the two are consistent or congruent the speaker is more likely to mean what he is saying and therefore more likely to be seen as genuine. Where inconsistency is perceived, the speaker is less likely to be regarded as trustworthy.

The Importance of Non-verbal Behaviour

In Chapter 8 on writing reports, the point was emphasised that it is as important to be aware of how something is written, as what is written. The same is true of conveying respect, empathy and genuineness. It is as important to be aware of *how* something is said, as *what* is said. In this way our non-verbal behaviour is an essential feature of how effectively we communicate with parents. It is an area which has been the subject of much research in recent years, with its effects in managing children's classroom behaviour being recognised increasingly (see Bull and Solity, 1987; Robertson, 1981). The major components of non-verbal behaviour are:
— posture,
— eye contact,
— inter-personal distance.
— gesture,
— touch,
— vocalisations.

Their combined effects contribute to the overall impression parents gain about teachers. Being aware of our own non-verbal behaviour can help in communicating respect, empathy and genuineness to parents. It is possible to think of what our posture might be, our gestures, eye contact, etc., when we are conveying these attributes. For example, teacher and parent might sit next to each other on chairs of the same height (rather than the teacher sitting behind her desk on a higher chair than the parent). Posture, eye contact and gestures would follow appropriately from the teacher's genuine interest and involvement in what the parents were saying.

SUMMARY

This chapter has drawn attention to some of the pitfalls in parent–teacher interactions and described important elements of a positive working relationship. Some of the more observable features are summarised in Table 9.2.

Table 9.2
Some Important Aspects of Discussions With Parents

Establishing common goals
Active listening
Staying silent when there is a pause
Asking for information
Clarifying assumptions
Summarising
Helping to identify parents' feelings
Getting the small things right

The principal aim when working with parents is to recognise the importance of establishing common goals. Although each party has a different starting point, both parents and teachers have the child's interests at heart. The aim of involving the parents of children with difficulties should be to reach an agreement as to the goals to which parents and teachers can jointly aspire whilst recognising the differences that may exits.

Active listening is indeed an *active* process and an essential component of the interview. Non-verbal behaviour such as body posture, eye contact and gesture also contribute in conveying to parents that a teacher is interested and involved in what is being discussed.

Pauses may well be helpful in enabling parents to collect their thoughts and find an appropriate way of expressing their feelings. The teacher needs to register whether he is jumping in too quickly during pauses or giving parents the necessary space to formulate and articulate their own views.

When information is sought, how are questions phrased? Are they the 'open' variety which give parents scope to express their opinions or are they 'closed', inviting only brief responses? Both can be appropriate, but will be so at different times.

In what areas are parents being asked to offer information? Are they being asked questions which place them in a position where only one, predictable answer can follow? This aspect of questioning needs to be monitored carefully during discussions to ensure a constructive interchange of information.

Assumptions will need clarifying as will certain details of parents' descriptions of events. Sometimes this will take the form of specific, concrete examples which help create a vivid picture of parents' perceptions.

Every so often during discussions, the teacher should summarise what she thinks has been communicated to her, just to check that her understanding is consistent with the meaning intended by the parent.

A teacher might also help to identify parents' feelings and reactions to the events they encounter. It is likely they will concentrate on descriptions of things that have happened, without relating these to how they felt as a result.

Finally, the teacher needs to monitor whether they will have created positive first impressions with parents. Are they likely to visit school feeling accepted and welcomed? Has care been taken in arranging the room where discussions will take place to ensure it is compatible with the climate of discussion you wish to create.

Perhaps the best way of assessing how things are going is to try and put yourself in the position of the parent and attempt to construe the situation from their side. Our aim should be to evolve a relationship in which parents feel accepted, valued, listened to and treated as equal partners in the process of identifying the child's needs and resolving difficulties.

Through examining and being aware of their own attitudes, values, strengths and vulnerabilities, teachers will enhance the quality of their relationships with parents and be sensitive to their needs. They will be in a better position to appreciate the sense which parents are making of events and to react constructively to ensure that their parental role is not negated, dismissed or undervalued. In this way parents and teachers can work together in an atmosphere of mutual acceptance and respect, in order to serve the best interests of the child.

FURTHER READING

Cunningham, C. and Davis, H. (1985). *Working with Parents: Frameworks for Collaboration,* Open University Press, Milton Keynes.
    Written for a range of professionals, including teachers, on the principles for establishing effective working relationships with parents.

Lansdown, R. (1980). *More than Sympathy,* Tavistock Publications, London.
    An informative paperback on the characteristics and needs of children with different handicapping conditions.

McConkey, R. (1985). *Working with Parents: a Practical Guide for Teachers and Therapists,* Croom Helm, London.
    Gives examples for how a successful partnership with parents can be developed and practical suggestions for working together.

Topping, K. (1986). *Parents as Educators: Training Parents to Teach Their Children,* Croom Helm, London.
    A comprehensive guide to projects involving the active participation of parents in their children's learning.

Wolfendale, S. (1983). *Parental Participation in Children's Development and*

Education, Gordon and Breach Science Publishers, New York.
Explores the potential for greater participation by parents in their
children's learning and proposes a framework for a working partnership
between parents and professionals.

Chapter Ten

LOOKING TO THE FUTURE

The nature of education is constantly changing and this is particularly apparent at the present time. This book is being concluded as a new session of Parliament is about to start (October 1987) and when the government is proposing radical legislation that could well dramatically alter the shape of existing educational provision.

A recurring problem facing authors of educational literature is deciding when to finish writing and submitting their work for publication. An inevitable concern is whether a book will still be relevant to the intended reader by the time it appears in print. Such an issue is especially pertinent about books which refer to educational legislation passed and introduced before 1988 which of course includes the 1981 Education Act. So how will future Acts of Parliament and government Circulars influence both in the short and long term, the identification of, and provision for, children with special educational needs?

THE NEW PROPOSALS AND CHILDREN WITH SPECIAL NEEDS

Five consultative documents have been issued by the DES which cover:
— a National Curriculum,
— schools deciding to 'opt out' of LEA control,
— parental choice of schools,
— financial delegation to schools,
— charges for school activities.
At the time of writing LEAs are being given an opportunity to consider the implications of the new Education Bill, but what is not clear is the extent to which the period of 'consultation' will lead to actual negotiated changes in the Bill between the government and those to be consulted before it is presented in the House of Commons.

The areas we would identify as carrying particular implications for children with special needs are first of all the impact of the proposed National Curriculum, secondly the repercussions of schools being given the opportunity to 'opt out' of LEAs, thirdly parental choice and finally schools having control of their own budgets. Many of the following statements are predicated by the word if. It remains to be seen what happens in practice.

The National Curriculum

It is proposed that there should be a core curriculum which all children follow. This will inevitably include basic numeracy and literacy, aspects of the curriculum where children frequently first come to the attention of their teachers as experiencing a difficulty in learning. What cannot be anticipated yet is the level of specificity with which attainment targets will be formulated, or the areas of study to be undertaken within each subject.

Linked to the National Curriculum are proposals for a series of 'bench mark' attainment tests to be undertaken by children of ages 7, 11, 14 and 16. Again the precise format of these tests is as yet unknown but they have nevertheless aroused strong feelings in many quarters as observers have questioned whether they signal a general return to a form of selective examinations reminiscent of those which were introduced following the 1944 Education Act (the Eleven Plus).

One might speculate as to the position of chidren who have been afforded the protection of a Statement of Special Educational Needs or those who will be subjects of the Statutory Assessment Procedure. What expectations will be held about their attainment levels and capacity to achieve at a level commensurate with their peers within the context of the National Curriculum?

'Opting Out'

Secondly, what will be the effects on children designated as having special educational needs when schools exercise their right to opt out of local authority control. If schools do opt out, what will be their position with respect to admitting a child with a Statement?

If a sizeable proportion of schools which remove themselves from LEA control were to decline to accept children with special needs, would not this result in the schools remaining within the LEA accommodating a larger proportion of children experiencing difficulties?

If judgements made by parents about a school are related to performance on nationally administered tests, then in all probability a statemented pupil is unlikely to achieve at a level *on those tests* which will enhance the school's overall results. Furthermore if some schools have a larger proportion of children with difficulties than others, they are likely to *appear* 'less effective' or 'less good', if how their pupils perform on the national tests becomes the single most important criterion by which a school is evaluated.

A further issue raised by schools 'opting out' concerns the procedures to be followed when complying with the Act. At present the Director of Education from an LEA has the responsibility of initiating the Statutory Assessment Procedure for determining whether special educational provision is required. Who would make these decisions if a school were not directly under an LEA? Similarly who would fulfil other roles in carrying out the legislation currently undertaken by LEA employees?

Parental Choice

Just as schools are likely to be given the opportunity of deciding whether to stay under the LEA or not, parents are also to be given increased choice in where their children are to be educated. Again, it is not clear where this will leave the parents of a statemented child. Will they, in reality, be able to exercise the same degree of choice as other parents (i.e. those with 'non-statemented' children), or will they be obliged to select from a limited range of alternative provision?

Financial Delegation

There are also likely to be significant implications for children with special needs of schools having greater control of their finances. Swann (1987) sees two particular consequences of this. One is that the integration of children with special needs into mainstream education is less likely to take place. Currently parents may direct their arguments in favour of integration towards LEAs who have some degree of flexibility in allocating funds. He anticipates greater difficulties in negotiating this aim with individual schools and the newly constituted LEAs.

Secondly, the formula by which a school's budget is determined may take into account the number of children on roll with Statements. Swann is concerned that there are no safeguards to ensure that resources offered are used for the expressed purpose of meeting the needs of children experiencing difficulties.

There are a large number of unknowns, many of which are unlikely to be resolved even when the legislation comes into force. It has for example taken a considerable period of time before the impact of major reports have been fully appreciated and assimilated. The implications of Plowden (DES, 1967), Bullock (DES, 1975) and Warnock (DES, 1978) are still being discussed today, albeit without perhaps the same intensity and passion as nearer the time of their appearance on the education scene. Whilst it may be relatively easy to implement some of the recommended changes in the new legislation quickly, their overall impact on the education of children with special needs may be less obvious and more difficult to interpret and anticipate.

IMPLEMENTATION OF THE EDUCATION ACT 1981

The best available guide to what might happen in the future comes from the Third Report from the House of Commons Select Committee (Volume 1) which has reviewed the implementation of the 1981 Education Act. The Committee sat between February and May 1987, visited three LEAs and invited witnesses from the professional bodies and organisations listed in Table 10.1

Table 10.1
Witnesses Appearing Before the Select Committee

Representatives of Hertfordshire, Sheffield and Derbyshire LEAs
Representatives from:
  University of London, Institute of Education
  National Union of Teachers
  National Association of Head Teachers
  Voluntary Council for Handicapped Children
  Society of Education Officers
  National Association of Advisory Officers for Special Education
  Department of Education and Science
  Her Majesty's Inspectorate of Schools

The Select Committee also received memoranda from a wide range of organisations, all with a keen interest in, and experience of, the 1981 Education Act. The following is a summary of the report, as it relates to ordinary schools, including some of its recommendations.

General Observations on the Implementation of the 1981 Act

The Committee concluded that a great deal had been accomplished since the Act came into force in April 1983:

> **The general thrust of the legislation has been accepted and there has been little call for radical revision of the Act.**
> **Paragraph 13**

It was further recognised that the Act had led LEAs and schools to pay greater attention to those children with special needs within mainstream education:

> **meeting special educational needs has become a more integral part of the work of primary and secondary schools.**
> **Paragraph 13**

Role of Parents

The Committee noted that:

> **although the Act, and the climate of opinion behind it, enhanced the position of parents in a way which is welcomed by LEAs and teachers, nevertheless there are still situations in which parents**

feel their contribution to the process of assessment has been insufficient or ineffective. The most common difficulties experienced by parents are:

(i) inadequate or unclear information about the LEA's assessment procedures and about the range of special educational provision available;

(ii) insufficient help in completing the parental contribution to assessment;

(iii) a lack of weight given to their views during the assessment process;

(iv) a lack of choice from a range of forms of provision.

Evidence also suggests that some parents who are members of ethnic minorities where the language of the home is not English, may find the formal procedure hard to understand.

Paragraph 16

The Committee recommended that voluntary organisations be encouraged and funded by LEAs to provide help to parents in dealing with schools and LEAs.

The Principle of Integration

The Committee recognised that there are different forms of integration. Where children with special needs are taught in special schools, it emphasised the importance of close collaboration between special and ordinary schools to ensure frequent interactions between their respective children. This was seen as one way of preparing children for the social demands of later life.

LEAs are encouraged to prepare:

a clear statement of its policy on integration, developed in consultation with parents and professionals, as part of its overall policy on special education. Parental choice is a necessary qualifier of, but not a substitute for, sensible strategic planning by an LEA.

Paragraph 19

The low morale of some staff in special schools was acknowledged and the Committee stressed that special schools, in their view, still had an important function, within an education system that advocated the principle of integration. It concluded the section on integration with the following statement:

to support the principle of integration is not therefore necessarily to support a principle of insisting that all children be educated in primary and secondary schools rather than special schools.

Paragraph 20

> Progress towards integrated forms of provision should now be
> evaluated both in terms of the quality of the educational provision
> and in terms of the wider appropriateness of the provision, so that
> greater guidance can be given to LEAs.
>
> **Paragraph 20**

Resources

The subject of resources raised two issues. The first concerned the
general lack of resources in schools, the second the lack of resources
available to implement the Act. The Committee noted that the question
of resources was raised most consistently by those submitting evidence.
This was also the concern identified most frequently by the teachers
with whom we have had contact during varoius in-service courses (see
Chapter 1).

The Act was brought into force without an accompanying
commitment to making additional resources available to schools and
LEAs. The Committee recalls that it was the view of the Government
that costs could be met from existing resources devoted to special
education, some of which would come from closing special schools.
However, although 147 special schools have been closed since January
1982, it has not been possible to determine the proportion of extra
resources being directed towards special education.

The Committee concluded:

> that the lack of specific resources has restricted implementation of
> the 1981 Act. A commitment of extra resources is needed if
> significant further progress is to be made.
>
> **Paragraph 23**

Definitions

The Committee stated that the new definitions:

> are relative, involving an individual child's relationship to the
> educational situations in which he or she is expected to function
>
> **Paragraph 24**

Three consequences of this definition were recognised:

> (a) that the better a school meets the range of individual
> difference in all the children who attend it, then the smaller will
> be the number of special educational needs which arise;

(b) the better a school meets the wider range of special educational needs which do arise, through the arrangements it makes and the services of the LEA generally available to all schools, then the less will be the number of children who may need to be the subject of statements;

(c) there will be variations in the extent of and provision for special educational needs from LEA to LEA. The evidence suggests that the relativity of the definitions is causing uncertainty and confusion.

Paragraph 24

A second area of difficulty relates to the way *special educational needs* are defined in terms of children having a *significant difficulty in learning*. The Committee identified four issues which emerged from the evidence:

(i) a learning difficulty is interpreted as poor achievement in traditional academic subjects and is not seen as an appropriate description of emotional and behaviour difficulties;

(ii) the concentration of the Act on procedures for making statements of needs and provision leads some to suggest that the Act's definitions do not include the wider range of special educational needs described in the Warnock Report;

(iii) the terms 'special needs' and 'special educational needs' are used in a variety of ways. The former phrase covers a much wider spectrum of a school's work including giftedness, English as a second language and social disadvantages, needs which in themselves may not give rise to special educational needs as defined in the Act. Some evidence suggests that all special needs which may require something additional or different in the nature of educational provision should be included in the Act;

(iv) some combined health and educational needs are, it is said, not adequately covered by the definition.

Paragraph 25

The Committee was against a *fundamental change* (our italics) in the definition of special educational needs, attributing the problems that have arisen to ones of interpretation and of relativity. They concluded:

there is a strong case for more guidance about identifying the wide range of special educational needs and about when a statement of such needs might be required.

Paragraph 26

A similar decision was taken about the definition of 'special educational provision'. The Committee felt there was uncertainty as to what constitutes such provision and recommended:

> that national guidance on such provision should be given.
>
> **Paragraph 27**

This arose because the duty of the LEA is to:
(a) secure that special educational provision is made in general terms (i.e. additional staff to primary and secondary schools, provide support teaching services and maintain advisory and psychological services), and
(b) arrange such provision for children for whom it maintains Statements. The second interpretation has been more widely accepted but DES information about the extent to which it is made suggests there is a:

> **wide variation among LEAs both in the percentage of pupils who are the subject of statements and in the percentage of these children who are having their needs met in primary and secondary schools.**
>
> **Paragraph 28**

The Committee concluded the DES should examine the reasons for this.

Meeting the Wider Range of Special Educational Needs

The Committee regretted that in some cases, where extra resources had been made available, these had been to increase administrative and psychological staff concerned with formal assessment. The evidence also suggested that in some LEAs, a preoccupation with the formal procedures had meant that meeting the wider range of special educational needs may not have received the attention it deserved. The Committee recognised:

> **there is a difficult borderline between what schools provide for all pupils and the special arrangements which they may make for some pupils with the wider range of special educational needs.**
>
> **Paragraph 30**

The Committee considered:

> **it unacceptable that there is such a lack of information about such provision and recommends that steps be taken to remedy the situation.**
>
> **Paragraph 30**

In the following Paragraph (31) the Committee concluded by saying:

> there is a case for the systematic allocation of teaching time,
> within primary and secondary school staffing ratios, to meet the
> wider range of special educational needs. In due course best
> practice on this question should be included in a DES Circular on
> staffing. These steps would reduce the current excessive pressure
> on authorities to carry out full assessments and to make
> statements.

Statutory Procedures for Assessment and Making Statements

The Committee acknowledged the general support for the
comprehensiveness of the assessment procedure, particularly the multi-
professional emphasis and the involvement of parents. However, a
number of problems were identified, relating to the time required to
complete the assessment, the complexity of the procedures, the
vagueness of Statements of needs and provision and that many
Statements of need are tailored to fit existing provision.

The Committee observed that:

> the period of time required to assess and prepare a Statement of a
> child's needs varies widely from area to area and this variation is
> not always related to the complexity of the case.
>
> **Paragraph 33**

The following are some of the suggested changes presented in evidence:

> (i)   a more streamlined procedure when professionals and
> parents agree on needs and provision;
> (ii) a time limit for the submission of professional reports;
> (iii) a time limit, of perhaps six months, for the completion of
> the process;
> (iv) more information and help for parents to make an effective
> contribution to the assessment process;
> (v)   access by parents to a named person, or befriender, who is
> not an employee of the local authority to assist them;
> (vi) steps to ensure that health authorities give sufficient priority
> to providing LEAs with necessary therapies recommended
> in statements.
>
> **Paragraph 34**

The Committee continues:

> We are in no doubt that aspects of the present system are not working satisfactorily. The weight of evidenc• shows on balance that it is the way these statutory procedures operate which is unsatisfactory, not their scope and purpose. The Committee recommends that the Department should examine closely ways in which procedures for assessment and making statements, could be improved. The Department should disseminate to LEAs examples of best administrative practice.
>
> **(Paragraph 36)**

National Arrangements for Promoting Good Practice

The Committee expressed concern at the way the implementation of the Act had been monitored by the DES. It recommends changes and urges the DES to offer greater guidance in the future.

Conclusion

The Committee end by stating that:

> the difficulties which arise are too wide ranging to be soluble by schools alone and too localised to be capable of close direction by central government. As a result, it seems to us that a successful implementation of the 1981 Act is very much dependent on the development by an LEA of a clear and coherent policy, arrived at in a way which enables it to command the support of those — parents, teachers and voluntary organisations — who are most affected by it.
>
> **Paragraph 50**

The impression conveyed by the report of the select committee is that the spirit of the Act and the educational principles underlying it, are valid and generally approved of. Any changes that occur are more likely to be concerned with tightening up key definitions, some of the administrative procedures and the anomalies that exist between LEAs.

Surkes (1987) in a recent headlined front page article in the *Times Educational Supplement*, reports that in reviewing the 1981 Act, the DES are basing their work on 'three DES-funded research projects, material from the select committee, and other information already received, including letters from parents'. The report suggests that the review would be unlikely to lead to a change in the Act itself but could produce revisions in the Circular 1/83.

This could mean that this Circular would be withdrawn entirely and replaced with another one, or, and this seems the most likely option, updated and clarified in line with some of the suggestions of the Select Committee.

THE SPIRIT OF THE ACT

Throughout this book we have attempted to capture what we perceive to be the spirit of the 1981 Education Act, the Regulations and Circular 1/83. Our interpretation has been based on our belief that, ultimately, it is the attitudes of teachers that will be more important in leading to the successful implementation of the Act than governments or politicians.

In Chapter 2 we highlighted six themes in special education which illustrate the nature of the changes that have already taken place within a relatively short period of time. That these developments have occurred, is itself a tribute to the combined efforts of all those who have worked tirelessly on behalf of children deemed to be 'handicapped' or 'disadvantaged' in the belief that they deserve a better deal.

The principles and practices described in this book are, we believe, in keeping with current trends in special education. The approaches discussed acknowledge the importance of identifying children's specific needs, through applying principles of education that serve to identify the needs of all the children in a class or school and not just those deemed to have special educational needs.

The model of assessment-through-teaching which we outlined in Chapter 6 is a non-labelling approach to identifying children's needs and the provision to meet them. It interrelates four key components within the process of education: *planning, teaching, learning* and *evaluation*. These underpin successful education and serve to unify what have, on occasions, been regarded as the separate practices of special and mainstream education, assessment and teaching.

We trust that readers of this book will accept that it is the responsibility of all who are involved in education to find ways of ensuring that children enjoy successful learning experiences, irrespective of the obstacles that may hinder us, as professionals. If our thinking about how to meet the needs of children remains flexible and open to new ideas, the outlook for our children will be healthy. Similarly, if teachers can accept being 'good enough' under prevailing political and economic constraints, they will enjoy a more satisfying professional life.

At this time of great uncertainty in education, what seems very certain is that the process of change continues. Let us hope that the changes resulting from the new legislation on special needs will genuinely benefit our children.

APPENDIX 1

(Taken from Annex 1, Circular 1/83)

ADVICE ON SPECIAL EDUCATIONAL NEEDS: SUGGESTED CHECKLIST

(a) DESCRIPTION OF THE CHILD'S FUNCTIONING

1. Description of the child's strength and weaknesses

   Physical State and Functioning
   (physical health, developmental function, mobility, hearing, vision)

   Emotional State
   (link between stress, emotions and physical state)

   Cognitive Functioning

   Communication Skills
   (verbal comprehension, expressive language, speech)

   Perceptual and Motor Skills

   Adaptive Skills

   Social Skills and Interaction

   Approaches and Attitudes to Learning

   Educational Attainments

   Self-image and Interests

   Behaviour

2. Factors in the child's environment which lessen or contribute to his needs

   In the Home and Family

   At School

   Elsewhere

3. Relevant aspects of the child's history

   Personal

   Medical

   Educational

(b) AIMS OF PROVISION

1. General areas of development

    Physical Development
    (e.g. to develop self-care skills)

    Motor Development
    (e.g. to improve co-ordination of hand and fingers, to achieve hand-eye co-ordination)

    Cognitive Development
    (e.g. to develop the ability to classify)

    Language Development
    (e.g. to improve expressive language skills)

    Social Development
    (e.g. to stimulate social contact with peers)

2. Any specific areas of weaknesses or gaps in skills acquisition which impede the child's progress
    e.g. short-term memory deficits

3. Suggested methods and approaches

    Implications of the Child's Medical Condition
    (e.g. advice on the side-effects of medication for epilepsy)

    Teaching and Learning Approaches
    (e.g. teaching methods for the blind or deaf, or teaching through other specialised methods)

    Emotional Climate and Social Regime
    (e.g. type of regime, size of class or school, need for individual attention)

(c) FACILITIES AND RESOURCES

1. Special Equipment
    (e.g. physical aids, auditory aids, visual aids)

2. Specialist Facilities
    (e.g. for incontinence, for medical examination, treatment and drug administration)

3. Special Educational Resources
    (e.g. specialist equipment for teaching children with physical or sensory disabilities, non-teaching aids)

4. Other Specialist Resources
    (e.g. Nursing, Social Work, Speech Therapy, Occupational Therapy, Physiotherapy, Psychotherapy, Audiology, Orthoptics)

5. Physical Environment
(e.g. access and facilities for non-ambulent pupils, attention to lighting environment, attention to acoustic environment, attention to thermal environment, health care accommodation)

6. School Organisation and Attendance
(e.g. day attendance, weekly boarding, termly boarding, relief hostal accommodation)

7. Transport

APPENDIX 2

(On preparing reports on children with special educational needs)

After reading Chapter 8, you may wish to apply the following questions to an advice which you may have prepared or one written by a colleague.

What do you think of the way the report is organised?

What impressions of the child are conveyed?

How much about the attitudes of the writer are revealed?

What do you think are good points in the advice?

Which parts of the advice (if any) do you find questionable?

To what extent are statements supported by relevant data?

To what extent could you say the advice is valid, reliable, fair, comprehensive and easily understood?

How have sources of information been attributed?

What impressions are conveyed about how the child responds to teaching?

What impressions have you formed about the child's strengths and weaknesses?

To what extent are the child's needs clearly specified?

What are your views on the provision identified as being most suitable to meet the child's needs?

To what extent has the writer appreciated the distinction between needs and provision?

What do you think of the way the views of the parents or child have been acknowledged?

Would you like your child to be written about in this way?

REFERENCES

Barker-Lunn, J.C. (1970). *Streaming in the Primary School*. National Foundation for Education Research, Windsor.

Becker, W.C. (1977). Teaching Reading and Language to the Disadvantaged — What We Have Learned from Field Research. *Harvard Educational Review* **47**, 518–43.

Becker, W., Englemann, S., Carnine, D. and Rhine, W. (1981). Direct Instruction Model, In W. Rhine (ed) *Making Schools More Effective, New Directions From Follow Through*. Academic Press, New York.

Beloff, H. (1980). A Balance Sheet on Burt, *Supplement to the Bulletin of the British Psychological Society* **33**.

Blankenship, C. and Lilly, S. (1981). *Mainstreaming Students with Learning and Behaviour Problems*. Holt, Rinehart and Winston, New York.

Block, N. and Dworkin, G. eds (1977). *The IQ Controversy: Critical Readings*. Quartet, London.

Bull, S.L. and Solity, J. E. (1987). *Classroom Management: Principles to Practice*. Croom Helm, London.

Burns, R. (1982). *Self-Concept Development and Education*. Holt, Rinehart and Winston, New York.

Cottam, P.J. and Sutton, A. (1986). *Conductive Education: A System for Overcoming Motor Disorder*. Croom Helm, London.

Cox, B. (1985). *The Law of Special Educational Needs: A Guide to the Education Act 1981*. Croom Helm, London.

Cunningham, C. and Davis, H. (1985). *Working with Parents: Frameworks for Collaboration*. Open University, Milton Keynes.

Department of Education and Science (1944). *Education Act*. H.M.S.O., London.

Department of Education and Science (1967). *Children and Their Primary Schools* (The Plowden Report). H.M.S.O., London.

Department of Education and Science (1975). *A Language for Life*, (The Bullock Report). H.M.S.O., London.

Department of Education and Science (1975). The Discovery of Children Requiring Special Education and the Assessment of Their Needs, Circular 2/75. H.M.S.O., London.

Department of Education and Science (1976). *Education Act*. H.M.S.O., London.

Department of Education and Science (1978). *Special Educational Needs*. (The Warnock Report). H.M.S.O., London.

Department of Education and Science (1981). *Education Act*. H.M.S.O., London.

Department of Education and Science (1981). *Education Act 1981*, Circular 8/81. H.M.S.O., London.

Department of Education and Science (1983). *Assessment and Statements of Special Educational Needs*, Circular 1/83. H.M.S.O., London.

Department of Education and Science (1983). *The Education (Special Educational Needs) Regulations*. H.M.S.O., London.

Elashoff, J. and Snow, R.E. (1971). *Pygmalion Reconsidered*. Jones, Ohio.

Engelmann, S. (1970). The Effectiveness of Direct Instruction on I.Q. Performance and Achievement in Reading and Arithmetic, *In* J. Hellmuth (ed) *The Disadvantaged Child* (Vol 3), pp. 339–61. Bruner-Mazel, New York.

Eysenck, H.J. and Kamin, L. (1981). *Intelligence: The Battle for the Mind*. Pan, London.

Fish, J. (1985). *Special Education: The Way Ahead*. Open University Press, Milton Keynes.

Gillie, O. (1978). Sir Cyril Burt and the Great I.Q. Fraud. *New Statesman*, 24th November.

Gipps, C. (1984). Issues in the use of standardised tests by teachers. *Bulletin of the British Psychological Society* **37**, 153–156.

Haring, N.G. and Eaton, M.D. (1978). Systematic Instructional Procedures: An Instructional Hierarchy, *In* N.G. Haring *et al.* (eds), *The Fourth R — Research in the Classroom*, pp. 23–40. Charles E. Merrill, Ohio.

Hewison, J., Tizard, J. and Schofield, W. (1982). Collaboration Between Teachers and Parents in Assisting Children's Reading. *British Journal of Educational Psychology* **52**, 1–15.

Insel, P. and Jacobson, L. (1975). *What do You Expect?* Cummings, Menlo Park, California.

Jackson, A. and Hannon, P. (1981). *The Belfield Reading Project*. Belfield Community Council, Samson Street, Rochdale.

Kamin, L.J. (1974). *The Science and Politics of I.Q.* John Wiley, New York.

Leach, D.J. and Raybould, E.C. (1977). *Learning and Behaviour Difficulties in School*. Open Books, London.

Levy, P. and Goldstein, H. (1984). *Tests in Education: A Book of Critical Reviews*. Academic Press, London.

Newell, P. (1983). *A.C.E. Special Education Handbook — The New Law on Children with Special Needs*. Advisory Centre for Education, London.

Pearson, L. and Tweddle, D.A. (1984). The Formation and use of Behavioural Objectives. *In* D. Fontana (ed) *Behaviourism and Learning Theory in Education*. British Journal of Educational Psychology Monograph Series No. 1, Scottish Academic Press, Edinburgh.

Postman, N. and Weingartner, C. (1969). *Teaching as a Subversive Activity*. Penguin, Middlesex.

Raybould, E.C. (1984). Precision Teaching: Perspectives, Principles and Practice. *In* D. Fontana (ed) *Behaviourism and Learning Theory in Education*. British Journal of Educational Psychology Monograph Series No. 1, Scottish Academic Press, Edinburgh.

Raybould, E.C. and Solity, J.E. (1982). Teaching with Precision. *Special Education/Forward Trends* **9**, 9–13.

Robertson, J. (1981). *Effective Classroom Control*. Hodder and Stoughton, Kent.

Rodgers, R. (1986a). *Caught in the Act: What L.E.A.s Tell Parents Under the 1981 Education Act*. The Spastics Society, London.

Rodgers R (1986b). *Guiding the Professionals: A Survey of LEA Guidelines for Professionals of the 1981 Education Act*. The Spastics Society, London.

Rosenshine, B.V. and Berliner, D.C. (1978). Academic Engaged Time. *British Journal of Teacher Education* **4**, 3–16.

Sharron, H. (1987). *Changing Children's Minds*. Souvenir Press, London.

Simon, B. (1978). *Intelligence, Psychology and Education*. Lawrence and Wishart, London.

Simon, B. (1985). *Does Education Matter?* Lawrence and Wishart, London.

Smith, F. (1978). The Politics of Ignorance. *In* L.J. Chapman and P. Czerniewska, *Reading from Process to Practice*. Routledge and Kegan Paul, London.

Solity, J.E. (1988). Systematic Assessment and Teaching-In Context. *In* G. Thomas and A. Feiler (eds), *Planning for Special Needs*, pp. 186-208. Blackwell, Oxford.

Solity, J.E. (1988). Systematic Assessment and Teaching-In Context. *In* G. Open University Press, Milton Keynes.

Surkes, S. (1987). Opting Out May Hurt Special Needs Pupils. *Times Educational Supplement*, 23rd October.

Swann, W. (1982), *Unit 12, Psychology and Special Education*. The Open University, Milton Keynes.

Swann, W. (1987). The Educational Consequences of Mr. Baker. *Special Children*, September, pp. 18-19.

Tomlinson, S. (1982). *A Sociology of Special Education*. Routledge and Kegan Paul, London.

Topping, K. (1983). *Educational Systems for Disruptive Adolescents*. Croom Helm, London.

Topping, K. (1986). *Parents as Educators, Training Parents to Teach Their Children*. Croom Helm, London.

Topping, K. and Wolfendale, S. (eds) (1985). *Parental Involvement in Children's Reading*. Croom Helm. London.

Wedell, K. (1973). *Learning and Perceptuo-Motor Disabilities in Children*. John Wiley, London.

INDEX